Fun with English

Fun with English

Sujata Patnaik

ALLIED PUBLISHERS PVT. LTD.

New Delhi • Mumbai • Kolkata • Chennai • Bangalore • Hyderabad

ALLIED PUBLISHERS PRIVATE LIMITED

D-5, Sector-2, **Noida**–201 301
Ph. Nos.: 0120-4320295/2542557/4352866
E-mail: delhi.books@alliedpublishers.com

17 Chittaranjan Avenue, **Kolkata**–700072
Ph.: 033-22129618 • E-mail: cal.books@alliedpublishers.com

15 J.N. Heredia Marg, Ballard Estate, **Mumbai**–400001
Ph.: 022-42126969 • E-mail: mumbai.books@alliedpublishers.com

No. 25/10, Commander-in-Chief Road, Ethiraj Lane (Next to Post Office)
Egmore, **Chennai**–600008
Ph.: 044-28223938 • E-mail: chennai.books@alliedpublishers.com

P.B. No. 9932, No. 15, 3rd Floor (Next to Vijaya Bank), 5th Cross, Gandhinagar, Karnataka, **Bangalore**–560009. Ph.: 080-41530285 / 22386239
E-mail: bngl.journals@alliedpublishers.com / apsabng@airtelmail.in

Sri Jayalakshmi Nilayam, No. 3-4-510, 3rd Floor (Above More Super Market)
Barkatpura, **Hyderabad**–500027
Ph.: 040-27551811, 040-27551812 • E-mail: hyd.books@alliedpublishers.com

Website: www.alliedpublishers.com

ISBN: 978-93-90951-61-1

Published by Sunil Sachdev and printed by Ravi Sachdev
at Allied Publishers Pvt. Ltd., D-5, Sector-2, Noida–201 301

Author's Note

I have always been fascinated by the dulcet tones of various languages and words. As a growing child, having been exposed to the rich nuances of speech in English and pursuing it as a part of academics, it was obvious I'd develop a passion for learning the ins and outs of the widely spoken language. Later on, years of teaching English prose, poetry and grammar in a college enriched my experiences, giving me an insight into the genuine problems a student encounters while picking up the intricacies of a 'foreign' language.

During the course of my scholastic study, I'd developed the habit of jotting down amusing pieces of language usage and other trivia from various newspapers, magazines, word-power books, the internet besides self-explanatory school texts. This habit found further expression and widening of horizons in my mental canvas throughout my teaching career. I began to collate and maintain notes on whatever information I could lay my hands on, no matter what the source. The habit of referring to a good dictionary was instilled by my English literature teacher right in Secondary school and I still adhere to this practice. Later on, I diligently began to follow the Thesaurus in order to improve my diction while writing for magazines and books. English newspapers, news bulletins and films have often provided the requisite impetus on this seemingly endless journey of learning.

With the popularity and necessity of learning and improving of English language skills, I felt it was high time I tried to bring out an interesting book from this vast ocean of knowledge based on the rich and varied aspects of English usage that will not only be useful to the readers but also entertain and amuse them. Since I haven't maintained formal records of all my notes or jottings, I would like to acknowledge and thank all the authors/publishers who have enriched my learning and helped me in disseminating the same. However, some of the time-tested books that have aided me in my efforts are 'A Second Book of English Idioms' of Orient Longman; 'Test Your Word Power' (Paperfront); 'A Treatise on the Art of Expansion and Precis Writing' (O.N. Gupta).

I hereby express my earnest gratitude to all the authors whose works have assisted me in my endeavor to bring out this informative book and hope my efforts will inspire the readers when they flip the pages within. I have, on my part, tried to keep a simple and, comprehensive approach so that a neo-learner too can benefit from it. I am thankful to Mr. Ravi Sachdev of Allied Publishers for having brought out my book. Last but not the least, I express my earnest indebtedness to Mr. Jagdish Singh of Allied Publishers for his encouragement and courtesy.

Sujata Patnaik

Contents

CHAPTER 1

Introduction

When we want to communicate our thoughts and feelings to others, we use a language as a mode of expression. Language, a word derived from 'Lingua' meaning tongue, is basically nothing but a vehicle of thoughts, a system of conveying or exchanging our opinions. It is believed man started using language 42,000 years ago. More than 5000 languages and dialects are spoken across the world today. Of the thousands of variegated languages followed globally, English has become the major 'Lingua Franca' i.e. the language that has been adopted as a common mode of communication between speakers of different cultural backgrounds. Although 360 million people are native English speakers, 1.5 billion or 150 crore people across the globe can speak English. Earlier, almost four centuries ago, English speaking people inhabited the present-day area of Great Britain. One in a hundred persons in the world used English then. But presently, one in every seven is well-versed in the language. The present age, with its digital precision and global competition has made communicative skills in English indispensable.

Out of almost three thousand spoken languages in the world presently, English happens to be the most global and influential one. The English vocabulary consists of over 5 lakh words. About 80,000 words are used in everyday speech. English is the native tongue in Great Britain, Ireland, the United States of America, Canada, Australia and New Zealand. English is the native, official or semi-official 'Lingua Franca' in more than forty countries across the globe. Inhabitants of several European, Asian, Latin American and African countries also understand and use the Queen's language which happens to also be the language of the world's postal services, trade and shipping and international aviation. International negotiations on environmental issues, wildlife protection, trade and commerce are mostly carried out in English. None can dispute the predominance of English in this electronic age of Information Technology and Telecommunication where computers, internet, e-mails, tablets, i-pods and other gizmos and gadgets rule the roost.

Scientific and medical research papers as also technical journals and books are more often published in English or translated into the language from the vernacular. More than 50% of the books in the world are in English, 66% of all scientific papers and technical books are published in English. Literary classics and masterpieces in global literature get due recognition and exposure by virtue of their English translation. Asia's first Nobel Laureate Gurudev Rabindranath Tagore's 'Gitanjali' fetched him the unique honor for Literature in 1913 mainly because of his translation of the original Bengali poems into English. W.B. Yeats, the eminent poet suggested to Tagore that for better prospects, he should first translate the poems into English. Yeats then proceeded to write the introduction to the book which subsequently won the Nobel and got translated into several other tongues. The large vocabulary of English is the outcome of the language's ability to adopt, embrace and absorb words from other tongues too, enabling it to evolve over the years.

Geetanjali Shree, an Indian author in Hindi won the prestigious International 2022 Booker Prize for her 2018 novel 'Ret Samadhi' that got translated into English as 'Tomb of Sand' by Daisy Rockwell. Hindi, with 60 crore speakers, happens to be the third most spoken language in the world after English and Chinese Mandarin that has 110 crores.

India is a multi-linguistic mosaic where the Indian constitution recognizes 22 languages. English remains the go-to language for different set of people who can't converse in a common language that is comprehensible to the different people. For people of most States, English is a voluntarily adopted link language as a medium of communication. Indian tongues too have adopted English words and phrases into their sentences as a part of routine communication. According to the census data of India, there are 1,635 rationalised mother tongues, 234 identifiable mother tongues and 22 major languages in the country. Pidgin English is rampantly used to overcome linguistic barriers among communities who find it difficult to imbibe the intricacies of English speech.

All said and done, English for us in India, an erstwhile British Colony, comes more spontaneously when compared to other languages like Spanish or French. People interact in mainly 13 languages throughout the world—Spanish, Italian, French, Russian, Arabic, Portuguese, etc. The most complicated language is Chipway, that Red Indians converse in. English, known to be an eccentric language has its own set of idiosyncracies that baffle the neo-learner. A punctuation mark, wrongly placed in a sentence can change the meaning totally. A comma, between words, a semi-colon or a full stop lends clarity to the meaning of the sentence. Many of us are unaware of the fact that the Question mark (?) came into existence only during the 15th century. An Italian, Aldus Manituvus (1450–1515) invented it but it is not known how he gave it the shape (?) as we know it today. Vagaries of English language with regard to its spelling, pronunciation, phrasal verbs, idiomatic expressions, undoubtfully, make for an amusing read.

Words having the same pronunciation are often spelt differently. Orthography, the conventional spelling system rattles non-English folks. For instance, 'mail', 'fail', 'sail', 'rail' are spelt alike and sound similar, yet 'scale' is never ever spelt scail. Technology has changed the way a word is spelt in modern English. GR8 stands for great, U for you, B4 for before are some shortcuts. 'Cite', 'site', 'sight' sound similar but are so dissimilar in meaning. You may have a 'dutiful' son but his wife can't be a 'butiful' daughter-in-law. The words 'look' and 'see' mean the same but when the prefix 'over' is placed before them they become opposites—'overlook' and 'oversee'. Even, for one having a flair for a plethora of languages, English ends up as a tough nut to crack. Understanding and interpreting phrasal verbs can be a nerve-wracking experience for a newbie.

Merely adding prepositions like 'in', 'on', 'up', 'for' to a verb 'call' will change the meaning in a sentence in each case, e.g. you call on (visit) a friend, call in (summon) a doctor in an emergency, call for (demand) an explanation, call up (recollect) events of your childhood, call off (cancel) the strike, etc. Multi-word verbs where an adverb particle or preposition is added to a verb are called phrasal verbs and can often create confusion for a greenhorn. For instance, we say: The war broke out (began) in 1914. The chief guest gave away (distributed) the prizes. You must learn to stand up for (defend) yourself.

The erratic pattern of forming the Past tense of a verb may leave a novice utterly flummoxed. If teach becomes taught, reach ought to become raught, preach logically should become praught. If peel becomes peeled in the past tense, can feel change to feeled? Oh, no. If dacoits 'looted' a bank, can we say a director 'shooted' the film in Iceland?

Since there is no consistent pattern in changing the gender, number or tense, learners of English language find themselves groping for the proper syntax and appropriate diction.

In 'proper' English too, some words are bound by certain rules and have to be written in the particular order.

Why do we say, "Little green men," not green little men or 'Little Red Riding Hood'?

Adjectives in English follow an order that dictates:

> Opinion-size-age-shape-color-origin-material-purpose noun.

For instance: You can have a lovely little old rectangular green French silver whittling knife.

Why do we say 'ding-dong' not 'dong-ding' 'tick-tock' not 'tock-tick'?

The rule goes as:

> If there are 3 words, the order will go I, A, O. If there are two words then the first is I and the second is either A or O. 'King-Kong', 'mish-mash', 'tic-tac', 'flip-flop', 'tip-top', 'hip-hop', 'chit-chat', 'sing-song', 'ping-pong', 'dilly-dally,' 'shilly-shally'.

Famous Irish playwright George Bernard Shaw considered English a crazy language due to its weird pronunciation. He said wittily that in place of 'fish' we could use the term 'ghoti'. His logic was:

In the word 'enough', the last two letters 'gh' are pronounced 'f'. In the word 'women', the 'O' is pronounced as 'I' (wimen).

In the word 'nation', 'ti' gives out the sound of 'sh'. So Shaw concluded that 'fish' or 'ghoti' could well be the same.

Other discrepancies cited to prove the vagaries of English usage are: if dad becomes pop, can mom become mop? If a vegetarian eats vegetable, what does a humanitarian eat?

Idiomatic expressions can be confusing like in 'letting the cat out of the bag' there is no cat or bag but the expression means 'leaking out a secret'. If your sermonising does not produce any effect on the listener, you say your arguments did not 'cut any ice' where 'ice' doesn't come anywhere into the picture and cutting it is a far cry.

And then there are some words which denote their non-existence. For instance, pineapple is neither a pine nor an apple, no ham in hamburger, no egg in eggplant. Guinea pig is neither from Guinea nor is it a pig.

Parts of speech, Figures of speech, Direct or Reported speech evoke confusing images in the English user's consciousness. Parts of speech are the basic introductory lessons one learns in grammar—nouns, pronouns, adjectives, verbs, adverbs, prepositions, conjunctions, interjections. Figures of speech comprise simile, metaphor, hyperbole, personification, irony, onomatopoeia, alliteration, etc. that are used to produce a rhetorical effect in the style.

Direct speech happens to be the style of presenting the exact words of the speaker using inverted commas whereas Reported speech tells what someone said but does not use the person's actual words. Hence no quotation marks are used.

Having taught the basic parts of speech in the initial classes of the higher secondary students, I asked them later about the number of Parts of speech in English. Of the few hands that were raised, I asked one girl who stood up with aplomb and confidently answered, "Two ma'am, Direct and Indirect." I was indeed stumped!

CHAPTER 2

Similes

A Simile is a figure of speech where one thing is compared to another. Some common similes are:

1. As blind as a bat
2. As bold as brass
3. As bright as a new shilling/ a button
4. As clean as a whistle
5. As cold as charity
6. As crooked as a corkscrew
7. As dead as the Dodo
8. As frisky as a lamb
9. As good as gold
10. As greedy as a pig
11. As high as a kite
12. As hot as hell
13. As hungry as a hunter
14. To kick like a horse
15. As old as the hills
16. As scared as a rabbit
17. As sharp as a knife/razor
18. As sick as a dog
19. As sly as a fox
20. As soft as silk/velvet
21. As strong as a bull
22. As stubborn as a mule
23. As timid as a mouse
24. As dry as a bone/dust
25. As brittle as glass
26. As little as a squirrel
27. As sincere as sunlight
28. As mischievous as a kitten
29. As honest as a mirror
30. As glorious as the morning
31. As straight as an arrow
32. As hard as iron
33. As flat as a pancake
34. As dull as ditchwater
35. As keen as mustard
36. As fierce as a lion
37. As sensitive as flowers
38. As beautiful as a rainbow
39. As proud as a peacock
40. As clear as crystal/daylight
41. As eager as a bridegroom
42. As simple as a child
43. As sacred as a shrine
44. As costly as an election
45. As tireless as the canoe
46. As opposite as poles
47. As swift as a thought
48. As unstable as the wind
49. As restless as ambition

50. As mysterious as the echo
51. As brilliant as the stars
52. As senseless as stones
53. As yellow as sulphur
54. As tough as leather/nails
55. As noiseless as a shadow
56. As obedient as a puppet
57. As tender as tears
58. As punctual as spring
59. As strange as a vision
60. As cool as a cucumber
61. As white as a ghost/a sheet
62. As busy as a bee
63. As black as coal/ink/pitch
64. As bright as the moon
65. As wise as an owl
66. As light as a feather
67. As heavy as lead
68. As quick as lightning
69. As sharp as a needle
70. As big as an elephant
71. As fit as a fiddle
72. Some similes that express coldness are:
    (a) As cold as a tomb
    (b) As cold as a ramrod
    (c) As cold as a frog
    (d) As cold as clay
    (e) As cold as a turtle
    (f) As cold as Greenland's icy mountains
    (g) As cold as the drifting snow

CHAPTER 3

Phobias

Have you heard the word 'Alliumphobia'? What does that mean? Well, it is the fear of 'garlic'. A Phobia is an irrational and debilitating fear of a certain object or situation. Some other phobias are:

1. Fear of animals – Zoophobia
2. Fear of strangers – Xenophobia
3. Fear of snakes – Herpetophobia
4. Fear of cats – Ailurophobia
5. Fear of dogs – Cynophobia
6. Fear of spiders – Arachnophobia
7. Fear of ghosts – Phasmophobia
8. Fear of air/flying – Aerophobia
9. Fear of darkness – Scotophobia/Nyctophobia/Achluophobia
10. Fear of blood – Hematophobia/Hemophobia
11. Fear of bad men – Scelerophobia
12. Fear of marriage – Gamophobia
13. Fear of fear – Phobophobia
14. Fear of crossing streets – Dromophobia
15. Fear of open spaces – Agoraphobia
16. Fear of closed spaces – Claustrophobia
17. Fear of smiles – Blennophobia
18. Fear of heights – Acrophobia
19. Fear of pain – Algophobia
20. Fear of water – Hydrophobia
21. Fear of trees – Dendrophobia

22. Fear of dead bodies – Necrophobia
23. Fear of work or being active – Ergophobia
24. Fear of injections – Trypanophobia
25. Fear of women – Gynophobia
26. Fear of certain sounds – Phonophobia
27. Fear of being stared at – Scopophobia
28. Fear of falling from a height – Bathophobia
29. Fear of crossing of bridges – Gephyrophobia/ Gephydrophobia
30. Fear of doctors – Latrophobia
31. Fear of heaven – Uranophobia/ Ouranophobia
32. Fear of wealth – Chrematophobia/ Chrometophobia
33. Fear of purple – Porphyrophobia
34. Fear of gold – Aurophobia
35. Fear of dining/ dinner conversation – Delpnophobia
36. Fear of hell – Hadephobia/Stygiophobia
37. Fear of thinking – Phronemophobia
38. Fear of kissing – Philemaphobia/ Philematophobia
39. Fear of vegetables – Lachanophobia
40. Fear of mirrors – Catoptrophobia/ Spectrophobia
41. Fear of sitting – Thaassophobia/ Kathisophobia
42. Fear of monotony – Homophobia
43. Fear of sleep – Hypnophobia
44. Fear of illness – Nosophobia
45. Fear of beards – Pogonophobia
46. Fear of nudity – Gymnophobia
47. Fear of high buildings – Batophobia
48. Fear of lists – Pinaciphobia

49. Fear of the number 13 – Triskaidekaphobia
50. Fear of stairs/slopes – Bathmophobia
51. Fear of disease – Pathophobia
52. Fear of witches/witchcraft – Wiccaphobia
53. Medical term for the fear of long words – Hippopotomonstrosesquippedaliophobia
54. Fear of insects – Entomophobia
55. Fear of snakes – Ophidiophobia
56. Fear of people – Demophobia
57. Fear of mobs/crowds – Ocholophobia
58. Fear of being robbed – Harpaxophobia
59. Fear of study – Logophobia
60. Fear of fire – Pyrophobia
61. Fear of rain – Ombrophobia
62. Fear of bees – Melissophobia/Apiophobia/Apiphobia
63. Fear of thunder and lightning – Astrophobia
64. Fear of contamination and filth – Mysophobia
65. Fear of speaking – Lalophobia
66. Fear of one's home – Ecophobia
67. Fear of men – Androphobia
68. Fear of solitude – Autophobia
69. Fear/hatred of books – Bibliophobia
70. Fear of sunlight or bright light – Heliophobia

CHAPTER 4

Sounds of Animals

1. A dog barks
2. A cat mews
3. A duck quacks
4. A dove coos
5. A hen clucks
6. A frog croaks
7. An owl hoots
8. A seal barks
9. An elephant trumpets
10. A pigeon coos
11. A monkey chatters
12. An alligator bellows
13. A bat screeches/squeaks
14. A bear growls
15. A deer bleats
16. An eagle screeches
17. A fly/mosquito buzzes or whines
18. A grasshopper chirps
19. A goat/sheep bleats
20. A pig grunts
21. A cow moos
22. A bird chirps
23. A lion roars
24. A wild goose honks
25. A snake hisses/rattles
26. A donkey brays
27. A mouse squeaks
28. A hippopotamus growls
29. A horse neighs
30. A parrot squawks
31. A rabbit squeaks
32. A swan cries/trumpets
33. A whale sings
34. A wolf bays/growls
35. A squirrel squeaks
36. A hyena laughs
37. A fox snarls/whelps
38. An ape gibbers
39. A moose/bull/buffalo bellows
40. A crow caws
41. A bee hums
42. A bird chirps

Sounds by other objects:

1. Air/wind whistles
2. Leaves rustle
3. A chain clanks
4. A bell chimes/rings

CHAPTER 5

Collection of Animals-Groups

1. A pride of lions
2. A school of fish
3. An army of frogs
4. A parade/gang/herd of elephants
5. A gaggle of geese
6. A bed of clams
7. An army of caterpillars
8. A kettle of hawks
9. A congregation of alligators
10. A shrewdness of apes
11. A kindle of kittens
12. A murder of ravens/ crows
13. A coalition of cheetahs
14. A parliament of owls
15. A flock of birds
16. A loft of pigeons
17. A herd of cattle
18. A dray of squirrels
19. A bevy/party/muster/ ostentation of peafowls (peacocks/peahens)
20. A swarm of bees/locusts
21. A convocation of eagles
22. A chattering of starlings
23. A pack of hounds
24. A colony of gulls
25. A mustering of storks
26. A troop of kangaroos
27. A brood of chickens
28. An exaltation of larks
29. A leap of leopards
30. A watch of nightingales
31. A clamour of rooks
32. A flush of ducks
33. A clutter of cats
34. A skulk/earth of foxes
35. A sounder of boars
36. An unkindness of ravens
37. A mob/gang of meerkats

CHAPTER 6

People who Collect Various Objects

There are names for people who love to collect various objects:

1. One who collects books – Bibliophilist
2. One who collects postcards – Deltiogist
3. One who collects dolls – Plangonologist
4. One who collects coins – Numismatist
5. One who collects currency notes – Notaphilist
6. One who collects teddy bears – Archtophilist/Arctophile
7. One who collects shells – Conchologist
8. One who collects butterflies – Lepidopterist
9. One who collects key rings – Copoclephilist
10. One who collects autographs – Philographist
11. One who collects flags or banners – Vexillologist
12. One who collects recipes – Receptarist
13. One who collects stamps – Philatelist

CHAPTER 7

Song Words

Remember the nursery rhyme Sing a Song of Sixpence, pocket full of rye.

Four and twenty blackbirds baked in a pie…? Let's delve into some musical words:

1. Lyrics – words of a song
2. Solo – single performance in a song
3. Aria – solo in an Opera
4. Duet – song by two performers
5. Orchestra – musical performance
6. Stanza – verse in a song
7. Serenade – romantic song
8. Blues – sad song
9. Lullaby – song sung to enable children to sleep
10. Anthem – song sung on special occasions for a country or organization
11. Paean – song of praise or triumph
12. Hymn – song as a prayer to god
13. Cantata – a narrative through song
14. Staccato – a song in breaks performed with each note separated from the others
15. Catch – humorous version in a song
16. Encore – repeat of a performance
17. Epithalamium – song celebrating a marriage
18. Symphony – musical orchestra
19. Reprise – repeat of the same song

20. Dirge/Requiem – mournful song
21. Libretto – text of an Opera
22. Contralto – lowest female voice
23. Soprano – highest singing voice
24. Tenor – male Opera singer
25. Octave – eighth count
26. Tympani – kettledrums
27. Oboe – wood-wind musical instrument
28. Banjo – musical string instrument
29. Cello – large string instrument which you sit and play
30. Bow – stick-like instrument used to produce vibrations from string instruments
31. Clavicord – old type of piano
32. Tuba – trumpet
33. Prelude – beginning of a song
34. Coda – conclusion of a song
35. Overture – beginning of an Opera
36. Prima Donna – lead female singer in an Opera
37. Plectrum – instrument used to produce sound from a guitar
38. Pot-pourri – jumbled mixture of songs.

CHAPTER 8

Tongue Twisters

Try saying these words very quickly…

1. I saw a saw, I never saw such a saw.
2. Sea shells on the sea shore, she sells on the sea shore.
3. Betty Botter bought some butter but the butter was so bitter so Betty bought some more butter to make the bitter butter better.
4. Peter Piper picked a peck of pickled peppers. If Peter Piper picked a peck of pickled peppers, where's the peck of pickled peppers Peter Piper picked?
5. So it is in or it is on, be it in or on, be it as it is.
6. 'The sixth sick sheik's sixth sheep's sick' is said to be the toughest tongue twister in the English language.
7. Can you can a can as a canner can can a can?
8. I scream, you scream, we all scream for ice-cream.
9. Give Papa a cup of coffee in a copper coffee cup.
10. A big black bug bit a big black dog on his big black nose.
11. Bigger business isn't better business, but better business brings bigger rewards.
12. If two witches were watching two watches, which witch would watch which watch?

Have fun with friends asking them to repeatedly utter these tongue-twisters very fast.

CHAPTER 9

Palindromes

A Palindrome, one of the unique quirks in English, is a word or sentence that reads the same backwards and forwards.

Some simple palindromes are:

Mom, pop, madam, deed, kayak, nun, noon, peep, civic, Malayalam. Palindrome sentences:

- Able was I ere I saw Elba.
- Madam, in Eden, I'm Adam.
- Was it a car or a cat I saw?
- Ten animals I slam in a net.
- A man, a plan, a canal – Panama!
- Dammit I'm mad – Backwards is still Dammit I'm mad—palindrome.

CHAPTER 10

Alliterations

Alliterations are words beginning with the same letter and sound to make the phrase or sentence in a poem attractive.

Some commonly used Alliterations with their meanings are:

- Through thick and thin – through good and bad
- Spick and span – clean and tidy
- First and foremost – important and imperative
- Safe and sound – come out of a tricky situation in good shape
- Kith and kin – friends and relatives
- Penny wise, pound foolish – looks after small change but not particular about large amounts.

William Shakespeare's oft-quoted lines using Alliteration are:

'After life's fitful fever
Full fathom five thy
father lies.'

Samuel Taylor Coleridge in 'The Rime of the Ancient Mariner' uses Alliteration often eg.

'The fair breeze blew, the white foam flew,
The furrow followed free,
We were the first that ever burst
Into that silent sea.'

Other examples using Alliteration are:

- Many monkeys make mud-pies many Monday mornings!
- Sleds slide sideways on shiny snow.
- Snowmen smile silently.
- Wonderful wishes of a winter wonderland.

CHAPTER 11

Etymology—Why is it called that?

The study of origin or derivation of words is known as etymology.

Months of the year:

- January – From the Latin Januarius the month of Janus, a Roman God with two faces believed to guard entrances. One face looks back into the past and the other forward into the future.
- February – From Latin Februarius, a purification festival held in that month.
- March – From Roman month Martius, from the god, Mars.
- April – Perhaps from Latin aperire, to open i.e. season when flowers start to open.
- May – Latin Maius, from goddess Maia.
- June – Latin Junius from goddess Juno.
- July – named after Julius Caesar.
- August – named after Augustus Caesar.
- September – Latin Septem-seven, it being the seventh month of the old Roman calendar.
- October, November, December – were the eighth, ninth and tenth months.

Days of the week:

- Sunday – the day of the Sun
- Monday – the day of the Moon
- Tuesday – from Tiw, a Teutonic god of War
- Wednesday – from the god Woden or Odin, the supreme deity
- Thursday – from the god Thunor or Thor, the god of Thunder
- Friday – from Frigg, the wife of Odin, representing love and beauty in norse mythology
- Saturday – day of planet Saturn.

CHAPTER 12

Who are the Rulers?

1. Monarchy – Rule by a king or queen
2. Bureaucracy – Rule by officials
3. Anarchy – Rule by nobody; absence of a government
4. Theocracy – Rule by a deity or god or the church
5. Autocracy – Rule by an absolute authority
6. Democracy – Rule by the people
7. Plutocracy – Rule by the rich
8. Dulocracy – Rule by slaves
9. Gynarchy – Rule by a woman or women
10. Stratocracy – Rule by the military
11. Patriarchy – Rule by the father
12. Matriarchy – The mother as head of family
13. Hagiarchy – Rule by priests or saints
14. Aristocracy – Rule by noblemen
15. Dyarchy – Rule by two independent authorities
16. Oligarchy – Rule by a few
17. Triumvirate – Rule by three powerful people
18. Tyranny – Rule by a despot
19. Hierarchy – Rule by family descendents
20. Technocracy – Rule by technocrats
21. Gerentocracy – Rule by old people
22. Martial Law – Rule by a military commander
23. Kakistocracy – Rule by the worst citizens
24. Pantisocracy – A classless utopian society in which all are equal and all rule

CHAPTER 13

Ologies

1. Zoology – The study of animals
2. Oology – The study of birds' eggs
3. Psephology – The study of elections
4. Pomology – The study of fruit growing
5. Limnology – The study of lakes
6. Bryology – The study of mosses
7. Dendrochronology – The study of tree rings and their link with historical dating
8. Silvology – The study of forests
9. Vulcanology – The study of volcanoes
10. Toxicology – The study of poisons
11. Ornithology – The study of birds
12. Gerontology – The study of old age
13. Metrology – The study of weights and measurements
14. Cardiology – The study of the heart
15. Entomology – The study of insects
16. Odontology – The study of teeth
17. Philology – The study of languages
18. Etymology – The study of origin of words
19. Graphology – The study of character from handwriting
20. Rhinology – The study of the nose
21. Palaeontology – The study of fossils
22. Herpetology – The study of reptiles
23. Ichthyology – The study of fishes
24. Speleology – The study of caves

25. Ethnology – The study of races of mankind
26. Hypnology – The study of sleep
27. Meteorology – The study of weather and its forecasting
28. Agnotology – The study of culturally induced ignorance

Robert Proctor a historian of science at Stanford University in California coined it from the classical Greek 'agnosis' meaning 'not knowing' plus 'logy' a subject of study from Greek 'logos' word or speech.

29. Mycology – The study of fungi, a group that includes mushrooms and yeast
30. Archaeology – The study of human history through excavation of sites
31. Astrology – The study of the effects of stars on the life of man
32. Biology – The study of functions and phenomena of living things
33. Seismology – The study of earthquakes
34. Psychology – The study of mind
35. Sociology – The study of social problems and human progress
36. Virology – The study of viruses
37. Neurology – The study of nerves
38. Osteology – The study of bones
39. Cytology – The study of cells
40. Nephrology – The study of functions and diseases of kidneys
41. Osphresiology – The study of odour and sense of smell
42. Physiology – The study of how living things function
43. Opthalmology – The study of the eyes and its diseases
44. Oneirology – The study and interpretation of dreams
45. Ethology – The scientific study of animal behaviour especially with reference to habitat

46. Deltiology – The study and collection of postcards
47. Battology – Unnecessary repetition in speaking or writing
48. Enology – The study of wines
49. Exobiology – Science that deals with the search for and study of life elsewhere in the universe than the earth
50. Agmatology – The study and treatment of fractures
51. Agrostology – The study of grasses
52. Archology – The study of the origin of things/science of government
53. Aerology – The study of physical properties of atmosphere
54. Aristology – The art or science of cooking and dining
55. Bromatology – The study of food
56. Caliology – The study of birds' nests
57. Chrysology – Economic study of precious metals and their value
58. Dactylology – The study of sign language or the use of fingers for the deaf and mute
59. Hypnology – The study of sleep and hypnosis
60. Mellitology – The study of bees.

CHAPTER 14

Adjectives relating to Animals and Birds

1. Feline – cats; i.e. stealthy
2. Canine – dogs; i.e. faithful
3. Bovine – oxen, cows; i.e. dull and boring
4. Ursine – bears; i.e. hirsute
5. Leonine – lions; i.e. majestic
6. Equine – horses; i.e. speed
7. Simian – apes; i.e. monkey-like
8. Elephantine – elephants; i.e. gargantuan
9. Cervine – deer; i.e. gentle and graceful
10. Vulpine – foxes; i.e. cunning
11. Leporine – hares; i.e. agile and quick
12. Ovine – sheep; i.e. meek
13. Murine – mice; i.e. super speed
14. Asinine – asses; i.e. stupid
15. Lupine – wolves; i.e. stealthy
16. Aquiline – eagles; i.e. astute, discerning
17. Piscine – fish; i.e. fertile, lucky
18. Avian – birds; i.e. freedom, grace
19. Anserine – goose; i.e. friendships
20. Corvine – crows; i.e. boastful
21. Pardine – leopards; i.e. opportunistic, stealthy
22. Taurean – bulls; i.e. impetuous
23. Serpentine – snakes; i.e. lengthy; transformation
24. Zebrine – zebras; i.e. chequered
25. Accipitral – hawks; i.e. rapacious

Other adjectives and their qualities:

1. Feminine – women; i.e. gentle, caring
2. Masculine – men; i.e. macho
3. Infantine – children; i.e. innocent.

CHAPTER 15

Words related to Horses

1.	Trot	– Walk of a horse
2.	Canter	– Slow running
3.	Gallop	– Full speed
4.	Stallion	– Male horse
5.	Bridle	– Restraining headgear of a horse
6.	Paddock	– Wooden enclosure for a horse
7.	Stable	– Place where horses stay
8.	Hoof	– Hard bone outgrowth at the feet of a horse
9.	Derby	– Horse race
10.	Frog	– Horny wedge in the sole of a horse's hoof
11.	Mare	– Female horse
12.	Filly	– Young female horse
13.	Colt	– Young male horse
14.	Pony/Foal	– Young of a horse
15.	Cob	– Short-legged, stocky horse
16.	Lorimer	– Ironsmith who makes spurs and bits for bridles of horses
17.	Caparison/Trappings	– Ornamental covering of a horse
18.	Jib	– Refuse, stop short
19.	Neigh	– Sound made by a horse
20.	Whinny	– Low sound made by a horse
21.	Cavalry	– Troops on horses
22.	Ostler	– Attendant for horses at an inn
23.	Mustang/Bronco	– Wild horse in the U.S. plains
24.	Hack/Nag/Jade	– Old or worn-out horse
25.	Gelding	– Castrated male horse
26.	Knacker	– Buyer of old horses for slaughter.

Chapter 16

Types of Animals

1. Vertebrates – Having a backbone
2. Marsupials – Animals that carry their young ones in a pouch
3. Arboreal – Living on trees eg. Macaque
4. Terrestrial – Living on land
5. Crustacean – Hard-shelled animals
6. Pachyderm – Thick-skinned animal
7. Cetacean – Mammals of water
8. Nocturnal – Active by night
9. Diurnal – Active by day
10. Fossorial – Digging and living animals
11. Volant – Flying animals eg. Bats
12. Squids – Animals with tentacles
13. Squamates – Animals/reptiles with scales
14. Mammalian – Animals that feed their young
15. Reptilian – Animals that crawl
16. Troglodyte – Cave-dwelling animals
17. Biped – Two-legged animal
18. Quadruped – Four-legged animal
19. Ungulates – Hoofed animals
20. Ovoviviparous – Reptiles that retain the eggs inside the mother's body until they hatch.

CHAPTER 17

Measuring Instruments

Derived from Latin 'metrum', the suffix 'meter' means measure.

These instruments measure:

1. Lactometer – purity of milk
2. Seismometer – earthquakes
3. Altimeter – altitude
4. Galvanometer – electric (galvanic) currents
5. Hygrometer – humidity of air or gas
6. Pyrometer – high temperature
7. Chronometer – time
8. Echometer – duration of sounds
9. Ammeter – electric currents
10. Hyetometer – rainfall
11. Photometer – intensity of light
12. Anemometer – wind speed
13. Optometer – eyesight
14. Bathometer – depth of water
15. Calorimeter – amount of heat
16. Pedometer – distance travelled on foot
17. Manometer – elastic force/pressure of fluid
18. Macrometer – distant objects
19. Micrometer – small objects, small distances
20. Tachometer – velocity of machines or of motor boats
21. Barometer – atmospheric pressure
22. Spectrometer – wavelengths of electromagnetic radiation
23. Hydrometer – density of a liquid

24. Voltmeter – voltage between two points
25. Thermometer – temperature
26. Sphygmomanometer – blood pressure
27. Viscometer – viscosity of fluids
28. Watthour meter – electric energy
29. Wattmeter – electric power
30. Algometer – intensity of pain
31. Astrometer – relative brightness of stars
32. Dendrometer – height and girth of trees
33. Dynameter – telescope's magnifying power
34. Dynamometer – power
35. Pyranometer – solar radiation.

Chapter 18

Persons: Tools

1. Poet/author – Words
2. Carpenter – Saw
3. Cobbler – Awl
4. Surgeon – Scalpel
5. Wrangler – Lasso
6. Astronomer – Telescope
7. Lumberjack – Axe
8. Mason – Plumbline
9. Painter – Brush
10. Seamstress – Needle/Scissors
11. Bricklayer – Trowel
12. Picador – Lance
13. Toreodor – Sword
14. Plumber – Wrench
15. Farmer – Plow
16. Sculptor – Chisel
17. Navigator – Sextant
18. Blacksmith – Anvil
19. Composer – Notes.

Chapter 19

Persons: Place of Work

1.	Miner	– Quarry
2.	Physician	– Infirmary/Hospital
3.	Sculptor	– Atelier
4.	Footballer	– Gridiron
5.	Baseballer	– Diamond
6.	Musician	– Conservatory
7.	Researcher	– Laboratory
8.	Lawyer	– Chamber
9.	Judge	– Courthouse
10.	Carpenter	– Workshop
11.	Gladiator	– Arena
12.	Artist	– Stage
13.	Busker (performer in a public place)	– Street.

CHAPTER 20

Manias

A mania is a compulsive desire or craze for something. What do the following manias stands for?

1. Kleptomania – desire to steal
2. Nostomania – longing for home
3. Bibliomania – craze for collecting books
4. Megalomania – desire to have great power
5. Dipsomania – craving for alcohol
6. Agromania – desire to be alone
7. Metromania – compulsive desire to compose verse
8. Chirablutomania – obsession for excessive handwashing
9. Pyromania – craze for starting fires
10. Sophomania – obsessive about one's own wisdom
11. Chronomania – perfectionism in time maintenance
12. Dromomania – craze for wandering.

CHAPTER 21

Miles with Smiles

1. Giggle – smile especially by girls
2. Glee – radiant smile
3. Grin – smile showing the teeth
4. Chuckle – happy smile by anybody
5. Chortle – happy smile often by an infant
6. Guffaw – boisterous laugh
7. Titter – nervous laugh
8. Cachinnate – Loud laugh
9. Smirk – smug smile
10. Simper – deceitful smile
11. Paroxysm – roll-over laughter
12. Snigger – disrespectful smile.

Chapter 22

Some Favorite Oxymorons

English language is full of contradictions where two words seemingly opposites of each other are used together. Known as Oxymoron, the figure of speech is used in many phrases and sentences.

1. New tradition
2. Assistant Supervisor
3. Plastic glass
4. Uninvited guest
5. Highly depressed
6. Live recording
7. Authentic reproduction
8. Partial cease-fire
9. Limited lifetime guarantee
10. Elevated subway
11. Dry lake
12. True replica
13. Forward lateral
14. Standard options
15. Small crowd
16. Seriously funny
17. Found missing
18. Liquid gas
19. Fully empty
20. Open secret
21. Foolish wisdom
22. Social distancing
23. Working holiday
24. Exact estimate
25. Clearly misunderstood
26. Act naturally
27. Pretty ugly
28. Tragic comedy
29. Only choice
30. Original copies
31. Legal murder
32. Wise fool
33. Deafening silence
34. Same difference.

CHAPTER 23

Types of Walks

If Gait is the art of walking, Malacca a cane or walking stick, what is a Zimmer?

Zimmer is a metallic walking frame used by elderly persons.

1. Mince – walk in short steps
2. Stride – walk aggressively
3. Strut/Swagger – walk with pride
4. Sidle/Skulk – walk in a clandestine manner
5. Gambol/Flit – walk with agility
6. Crawl – walk on all fours
7. Catwalk – pretentious walk by fashion models on a ramp
8. Plod – walk heavily
9. Promenade – walk leisurely in a public place
10. Esplanade – walk along the seashore
11. Waddle – walk like a duck
12. Wobble – drunken man's walk
13. Infiltrate – walk into an area secretly
14. Traipse – walk wearily
15. Trespass – walk illegally into an area
16. Saunter/Ramble – walk aimlessly
17. March – walk to a rhythm
18. Meander – walk in a circuitous manner.

Chapter 24

Contronyms

Can a word be its own opposite?

Yes! They are called contronyms—words that happen to be their own Antonyms, according to their context.

1. Left – can mean both 'remaining' and 'departed'.
2. Dust – can mean 'to add fine particles' or 'to remove fine particles'.
3. Off – can mean 'activated' and 'deactivated'.

   E.g., Set off – activated

   Switch off – deactivated.
4. Screen – can mean 'to show' and 'to hide'.
5. Oversight – may imply both 'watchful care' and 'an inadvertent error'.
6. Sanction – can mean 'an official permission or approval for an action' or 'a penalty for disobeying a law'.
7. Transparent – can mean 'obvious' and 'invisible'.
8. Buckle – can mean 'to secure with a buckle' and can mean 'to bend' also.
9. Execute – can mean both 'to begin' as also 'to bring to an end.'
10. Put out – can mean 'extinguish' and 'generate'.
11. To clip – can be used 'to detach' as well as 'to fasten'.
12. To cleave – can mean 'to cling on' and 'to split'.

CHAPTER 25

Isms

What do these words ending in 'ism' mean?

1. Atheism – denial of the existence of a God
2. Deism – belief in God without proof or revelation
3. Baptism – religious rite of initiation into the church
4. Neologism – the use of new words
5. Plagiarism – using another person's thoughts or writing as one's own
6. Malapropism – a ridiculous misuse of a word usually for one resembling it
7. Cubism – the art style where objects are presented in geometrical shapes
8. Archaism – an old or obsolete expression
9. Criticism – fault finding
10. Hypnotism – artificially producing a state of deep sleep
11. Pantheism – the belief that all is God and god is all
12. Fatalism – belief that everything that happens is predetermined by fate
13. Chauvinism – exaggerated and warlike patriotism
14. Surrealism – art form representing dreams and the subconscious
15. Spoonerism – when corresponding sounds in two words are interchanged; a speech error
16. Altruism – regard for well-being of others
17. Masochism – enjoying an activity that appears painful or tedious

18. Colloquialism – an expression pertaining to common speech
19. Stoicism – endurance of pain without complaint
20. Euphemism – use of a mild expression instead of a blunt or offensive one
21. Somnambulism – walking in sleep
22. Agnosticism – belief that God's existence cannot be known or proven
23. Euphuism – Affected style of writing
24. Aphorism – A maxim; a concise expression
25. Teetotalism/ Nephalism – total abstinence from intoxicants
26. Transvestism – the practice that induces a person to wear clothes of the opposite sex
27. Polytheism – the belief in many gods
28. Pantheism – The belief that everything is godly
29. Alogism – An illogical statement
30. Jingoism – Attitude of extreme nationalism.

CHAPTER 26

Homonyms

Similar sounding words that differ in meaning are known as Homonyms.

Homonyms – Same sound or spelling but different meaning

Homophones – Same pronunciation but different meaning

Homographs – Same spelling words but differ in meaning or pronunciation

1. Drill – A tool
   Drill – A military exercise
2. Defile – To corrupt
   Defile – A narrow pass
3. Refrain – To abstain
   Refrain – A recurring verse in song
4. Lumber – To move heavily
   Lumber – Useless odds-and-ends
5. Crane – A large bird
   Crane – A machine for lifting things
6. Carp – A species of fish
   Carp – to find fault
7. Season – To mature or ripen
   Season – A period of the year
8. Corporal – A military rank
   Corporal – Relating to the body
9. Ash – The residue of burning
   Ash – A forest tree
10. Trifle – A small sum or amount
    Trifle – A sweet confection

Chapter 27

Famous Words Ending in 'Ice'

1. Solid form of water – Ice
2. A pale blue or green paint – Bice
3. Calling for very fine discrimination – Nice
4. The staple food of India – Rice
5. A little pig – Grice
6. The sap of vegetables – Juice
7. The amount payable to sell or buy anything – Price
8. A thin broad piece – Slice
9. An aromatic and pungent vegetable substance used as a condiment for seasoning food – Spice
10. Sound given out by anything – Voice
11. Specially skilled opinion – Advice
12. Act or power of choosing – Choice
13. A penetential garment made of haircloth – Cilice
14. Anything that is designed – Device
15. To induce by exciting hope or desire – Entice
16. Disposition or intention to harm another or others – Malice
17. One new in anything – Novice
18. A building used for a work place – Office
19. The system of regulations for the preservation of order and enforcement of law – Police
20. A frothy portion of any lava – Pumice
21. To join together by overlapping – Splice
22. The merchant of this city was very famous – Venice

23. Eager desire for wealth – Avarice
24. A change of humour or opinion without reason – Caprice
25. A projecting moulding along the top of a building – Cornice
26. A narrow opening – Crevice
27. Condition or occupation of a servant or of one who serves – Service
28. A disease in which there is yellowing of the eyes – Jaundice
29. A soft composition applied in a cloth to sores – Poultice
30. Reported performance as a means of acquiring skill – Practice
31. Want of courage – Cowardice
32. A high vertical or nearly vertical cliff – Precipice
33. Judgement or opinion formed beforehand or without due examination – Prejudice
34. One bound to another to learn a craft – Apprentice

CHAPTER 28

Ah! Ants!!

An ant can don many caps, indeed! Some specimens to enjoy:

1. A spy ant – informant
2. A proud ant – arrogant
3. Five ants + five ants – tenants
4. A small ant – infant
5. An ant you don't like – irritant
6. An ant that has good knowledge – brilliant
7. An ant on its legs – elegant
8. A brave ant – gallant
9. A victorious ant – triumphant
10. A big ant – giant
11. An ant that is found everywhere – abundant
12. A cool and friendly ant – coolant
13. An ant that looks different – variant
14. An ant that is quarrelsome – litigant
15. An ant in search of a job – applicant
16. A dirty ant – pollutant
17. A shouting ant – rant
18. An ant that holds on – adamant
19. An ant that flees to another country – migrant
20. An ant that comes to live in a foreign country – immigrant
21. An ant that thrives on leftovers – remnant
22. An ant brought from another country – important
23. An ant that doesn't want a change – reluctant
24. An ant that maintains financial records – accountant

25. An ant that is an advisor or specialist – consultant
26. An ant that occupies a flat – occupant
27. An unfriendly ant – distant
28. A large ant – elephant
29. An ant that remains stable – constant
30. A cruel ant – tyrant
31. An important ant – significant
32. A sarcastic ant – mordant
33. An ant that is quick – instant
34. An ant that activates you – stimulant
35. An ant that never stops – incessant
36. An ant vital in English words – consonant

CHAPTER 29

Interesting Play of Words Used as Nouns and Verbs

1. **Will** you have a provision for me in your **will**?
2. **Can** you please remove that **can**?
3. **Bow** your head to lift the **bow**.
4. **Bank** on a well wisher when you go to a **bank**.
5. **May** we arrive in early **May**?
6. **Fair** girls can be seen in the **fair**.
7. **Train** the children to carefully board a **train**.
8. **Dear** lady, diamonds are very **dear**.
9. **Rest** of the tired tourists desired to take some **rest**.
10. **Park** your vehicles outside the **park**.
11. When the **going** gets **tough**, the **tough** get **going**.

CHAPTER 30

Portmanteau (Pronounced port-man-toe)

A word blending sounds, combining the meaning of two others to form a new word. In short, two meanings packed up into a single word is a portmanteau.

Often the first segment of one word is combined to the final segment of another word to form a portmanteau. Its fun to spot some such words in use these days.

1. Smog is a portmanteau from smoke and fog.
2. Brunch – Breakfast and Lunch
3. Spork – Spoon and Fork
4. Podcast – iPod and Broadcast
5. Newscast – News and Broadcast
6. Infotainment – Information and Entertainment
7. Motel – Motor and Hotel
8. Oxbridge – Oxford and Cambridge
9. Permalance – Permanent freelance
10. Advertorial – Advertising and Editorial
11. Chortle – Chuckle and Snort
12. Biopic – Biography and Picture
13. Anklet – Ankle and Bracelet
14. Brexit – Britain and Exit
15. Emoticon – Emotion and Icon
16. Glamping – Glamorous and Camping
17. Guesstimate – Guess and Estimate
18. Internet – Interconnected and Network

19. Metaverse – Meta and Universe
20. Mocktail – Mock and Cocktail
21. Romcom – Romance and Comedy
22. Webinar – Web and Seminar
23. Wi-Fi – Wireless and Fidelity
24. Stagflation – Stagnant and Inflation
25. Dancercise – Dance and Exercise
26. Staycation – Stay and Vacation
27. Traincation – Train and Vacation (using a train instead of a car or aeroplane for travel)
28. Haycation – Hay and Vacation (holidays in rural homestays)
29. Phubbing – Phone and snubbing (awkward practice of ignoring those around while scrolling a mobile phone)
30. Foodpreneur – Food and Entrepreneur
31. Swicy – Sweet and spicy
32. Webucation – Web and education
33. Dramedy – Drama and comedy

Chapter 31

Some Funny Signboards

1. **In a Laundromat:** Automatic washing machines: Please remove all your clothes when the light goes out.
2. **In an office:** After tea break staff should empty the teapot and stand upside down on the draining board.
3. **Spotted in a safari park:** Elephants please stay in your car.
4. **In an office:** Toilet out of order...... Please use floor below.
5. **Notice on health food shop window:** Closed due to illness.
6. **On a repair shop door:** We can repair anything (Please knock hard on the door – The bell doesn't work.)
7. **In an office:** Would the person who took the step ladder yesterday please bring it back or further steps will be taken.
8. **Seen during a conference:** For anyone who has children and doesn't know it, there is a day care on the 1st floor.
9. **Notice in a farmer's field:** The farmer allows walkers to cross the field for free but the bull charges.
10. **Notice outside a secondhand shop:** We exchange anything – Bicycles, washing machines, television, etc. why not bring your wife along and get a wonderful bargain?
11. Some oddities are:
    (a) How is it noses run while feet smell?
    (b) People recite at a play but play at a recital.
    (c) How is it your house can burn up as it burns down?
    (d) An alarm goes off by going on.
    (e) You fill in a form by filling it out.
    (f) A boxing ring is not round but square, while quicksand far from being quick works slowly.
    (g) When I wind up my watch, I start it, when I wind up my work, I end it.

CHAPTER 32

Number: Singular-Plural

English is a crazy language and one comes across wonderful observations on formation of plural nouns, that differ vastly despite having similar type of spelling in the singular number.

If the plural of man is men, then the plural of pan should have been pen and not pans. The plural of box is boxes but ox in its plural form becomes oxen, not oxes. A lone foot but two feet, then one boot, should become beet as a pair but you have two boots. A single goose becomes several geese but by the similar utterance moose has its plural as moose only. A single mouse but several mice yet a single house doesn't give you 'hice' for several houses.

If a child cuts a single tooth, over a period of time he has several teeth but imagine a single booth having its plural as beeth. Brother can also be spoken as brethren in plural then why can't mother become methren? The masculine gender pronouns are he, his and him but the feminine are she, her and hers not she, shis or shim.

Some uncommon singular words in English have plural like:

1. Child – Children
2. Hero – Heroes
3. Bison – Bison
4. Thief – Thieves
5. Dwarf – Dwarfs
6. Roof – Roofs
7. Radius – Radii
8. Self – Selves
9. Larva – Larvae
10. Analysis – Analyses
11. Tomato – Tomatoes

12. Nucleus – Nuclei
13. Axis – Axes
14. Index – Indices
15. Stratum – Strata
16. Criterion – Criteria
17. Tornado – Tornados
18. Torpedo – Torpedoes
19. Graffito – Graffiti
20. Formula – Formulae/Formulas
21. Bureau – Bureaus
22. Crisis – Crises
23. Nebula – Nebulae
24. Phenomenon – Phenomena
25. Sister-in-law – Sisters-in-law
26. Stimulus – Stimuli
27. Genus – Genera
28. Datum – Data
29. Bacterium – Bacteria
30. Alumnus – Alumni
31. Agendum – Agenda
32. Louse – Lice
33. Moose – Moose

Some nouns are used in plural form only. e.g. spectacles, trousers, breeches, scissors

Whereas some nouns singular in form are always used as plural. e.g. gentry, people, cattle, alphabet, police.

CHAPTER 33

Ailments of the Body

Can you name the part of the body affected by the diseases mentioned?

1. Hepatitis – Liver
2. Colitis – Colon or Intestine
3. Gastritis – Stomach
4. Arthritis – Joints
5. Meningitis – Brain and Spinal Cord
6. Stomatitis – Mouth
7. Neuritis – Nerves
8. Conjunctivitis – Eye
9. Phlebitis – Veins
10. Dermatitis – Skin
11. Bronchitis – Lungs
12. Poliomyelitis – Spinal Cord
13. Glomerulonephritis – Kidneys
14. Pyorrhoea – Teeth and gums
15. Glaucoma – Eyes
16. Vertigo – Brain or inner ear
17. Quadriplegia – All four limbs

Chapter 34

Borrowed Words Commonly used in English

English borrows heavily from other languages like Latin, German, French, Spanish, Italian, etc. Hence it has a larger and more varied vocabulary than many other languages. Australia is derived from the Latin 'Terra Australis Incognito' or 'The Unknown Southern land…'

Onion gets its name from The Latin 'unio' meaning 'large pearl'.

Other **Latin** words in English:

1. *Ipso facto* – by the fact itself
2. *In toto* – completely
3. *Bona fide (bona fydy)* – genuine, in good faith
4. *Status quo* – the existing state of things
5. *Vice versa* – in reverse; conversely
6. *Ad lib* – as much as one likes; done or spoken without preparation
7. *Sine qua non* – absolutely necessary
8. *Ad infinitum* – forever, without end
9. *Tempus fugit* – time flies
10. *Infra dig* – beneath one's dignity
11. *Per se* – intrinsically; by or in itself
12. *Pro tem* – for the time being, temporarily
13. *Terra Firma* – dry or firm land as opposed to sea or air
14. *Per annum* – yearly
15. *Quid pro quo* – tit for tat, one thing in place of another

16. *Ultimo* – of last month
17. *Caveat emptro* – let the buyer beware
18. *In camera* – in secret, in a closed court
19. *Ex officio* – in discharge of duty/by virtue of his office
20. *Ultra vires* – beyond the powers or legal authority of
21. *Non-sequitur* – it does not follow
22. *pro rata* – in proportion to the value of
23. *A fortiori* – with stronger reason
24. *Sub judice* – under consideration of a court or judge
25. *Quid pro quo* – a favor or advantage granted in return for something
26. *Agenda* – things to be done
27. *de facto* – in existence
28. *Viz* – namely, in Latin 'Videlicet'
29. *Magnum opus* – masterpiece
30. *Prima facie* – at first glance
31. *Pro forma* – as a matter of form
32. *Vox populi* – voice of the people
33. *Ab initio* – from the beginning
34. *Ad nauseam* – a topic that is sickening or tiresome as it has been repeated very often.
35. *Sic* – so, thus... Adverb – sic – used in brackets after a quoted word that appears odd to show that the word is quoted exactly as it stands in the original, as in 'a story must hold a child's interest and enrich his (sic) life.'
36. *Circadian* is a latin word which means, 'About a day.' The 'Circadian Rhythm' refers to an internal or biological clock that regulates our sleep-wake cycle.
37. NB – note well, an abbreviation of latin *nota bena*, used to bring something to the attention of the reader

38. A.M. or a.m. – abbreviation for Latin '*ante meridian*', the period of time between midnight and midday
39. P.M. or p.m. – abbreviation for Latin '*post meridian*', period between midday and midnight
40. RIP – in Latin 'requiescat in peace' meaning may he or she rest in peace
41. e.g. – for example – from Latin 'exempli gratia'
42. i.e. – that is to say – from Latin id est
43. *Ex gratia* – pronounced exgraysha – of a payment made by a special decision
44. *Ibid* – Abbreviation for Latin 'ibidem' that means 'in the same place' or from the same source
45. *Dei gratia* – by the grace of god.

Derivative words from other languages:

French

1. *Adieu* – farewell
2. *aide-de-camp* – field aide
3. *a la carte* – according to the menu
4. *a la mode* – in the fashion
5. *bon vivant* – one who likes to live well
6. *communique* – official statement of dispatch
7. *coup de grace* – death blow
8. *coup de etat* – seizure of govt by sudden stroke
9. *de jure* – legally
10. *esprit de corps* – spirit of loyalty to one's group
11. *fait accompli* – things already done
12. *faux pas* – false step, blunder
13. *resume* – summary

14. *roulette* – gambling wheel
15. *sangfroid* – coolness in the face of danger
16. *Sans souci* – carefree, free from worry
17. *Double entendre* – (pronounced Doobla antundra) – a word or phrase open to two interpretations, one of which is usually indecent.
18. *de riguer* – (de reeger) – the quality of being unyielding. In English, it means necessary according to certain rules.
19. *avant garde* (pronounced avon gard) – people or ideas that are daringly modern in views or works.
20. *Faux Pas* (pronounced 'Fo pa') – False step, literally in French. A social blunder or a tactless act or remark.
21. *R.S.V.P.* – Please Reply, from the French phrase 'Répondez s'il vous plaît'.

Italian

1. *Bambino* – child
2. *fiasco* – failure
3. *manifesto* – declaration
4. *marina* – settled landscape and sea shore
5. *tutti frutti* – all fruits mixed
6. *volte face* – a reversal of opinion

Hindi

1. *Ahimsa* – doctrine of non-violence
2. *Cheetah* – spotted leopard
3. *Guru* – teacher
4. *Kama* – Hindu god of love
5. *Khaki* – dust coloured, dull-brownish-yellow fabric of cotton or wool

6. *Yoga* – Hindu system of philosophic meditation and asceticism designed to effect reunion with the universal spirit

Words of Indian origin like chit, jungle, bungalow, cushy, juggernaut, bandicoot, shampoo, pariah have been absorbed into common English usage.

Japanese

1. Hara-kiri – ceremonial suicide
2. Sayonara – goodbye
3. Samurai – Japanese feudal noble man

Miscellaneous

1. *Apartheid* – Dutch – South African policy of racial segregation.
2. *Kabab* – Persian – meat cooked/baked with spices usually on skewer.
3. *Robot* – Czech – Automaton trained to do man's work.
4. *zeitgeist* – German – spirit of the times.
5. *Panic-stricken* – Greek – Panic derived from the name of the Greek god Pan, protector of sheep and patron of shepherds. His horned head appearance with a goat's hindquarters scared everyone, causing 'panic fear'. 'Pan' signifies everything and was originally one of the eight gods of Egyptian mythology.
6. *hoi polloi* – (hoy poloy) Greek – common people
7. *apostolos* – Greek – messenger
8. *Buenos dias* – Spanish – Good morning.

Chapter 35

Spell Well

The word 'picnic' is often misspelt as 'picknick' just as 'newspaper' is spelt as 'newspapper', 'systemetic' for 'systematic'. Some commonly misspelt words are:

Incorrect	*Correct*
Recieve	Receive
Panick	Panic
Embarass	Embarrass
Vaccum	Vacuum
Philanthrophy	Philanthropy
Exhorbitent	Exorbitant
Supercede	Supersede
Defination	Definition
Harrass	Harass
Woolens	Woollens
Kindergarden	Kindergarten
Congrajulations	Congratulations
Collosal	Colossal
Tresspass	Trespass
Planetorium	Planetarium
Rishkaw	Rikshaw
Burow	Bureau
Diary farm	Dairy farm
Recepient	Recipient
Attendence	Attendance
Opressive	Oppressive
Occassion	Occasion
Obssesion	Obsession
Possesion	Possession
Heriditary	Hereditary

Chapter 36

Interesting Facts

The first English Dictionary was written in 1755 by Samuel Johnson. Called A Dictionary of the English language, it took over 8 years to compile, required six helpers and listed 40,000 words.

1. Pangrams – An English Pangram is a sentence that contains all 26 letters of the English alphabet.
   - Jackdaws love my big sphinx of quartz – A sentence in English containing all the 26 letters of the alphabet.
   - A quick hungry fox jumps over the lazy, brown dog – All 26 letters of the English alphabet.
   - Amazingly few discotheques provide jukeboxes – All 26 letters of English alphabet found in this small sentence.
2. The longest non-technical word in major dictionaries is FLOCCINAUCINIHILIPILIFICATION at 29 letters meaning – 'is the act of considering something to be worthless.'
3. 'I am' is the shortest complete sentence in the English language.
4. There are 5 words in the English language that have all five vowels in order 'Facetious', 'Abstemious', 'Abstentious', 'Arsenious', 'Arteriosus' – all vowels in order.
5. Cambodian has 74 letters, the longest alphabet as compared to 26 in English.
6. Colours denoting emotions:
   - Green – Jealousy
   - Blue – Spirituality/serenity
   - Red – Anger
   - Yellow – Cowardice
   - White – Purity
   - Purple – Royalty
   - Black – Mourning
   - Brown – Rustic

CHAPTER 37

Symbolisms

1. Sea – problems
2. River – thoughts
3. Ocean – knowledge
4. Torch – liberty
5. Scales – justice
6. Scythe – time
7. Weights – burdens, encumbrances
8. Nod – assent
9. Glower/scowl – anger
10. Sneer – contempt
11. Shrug – indifference
12. Crystal – clear
13. Clasp/Embrace – affection
14. Diamond – hardness
15. Zircon – brilliance
16. Unicorn – chastity
17. Sphinx – mystery
18. Phoenix – immortality
19. Salamander – tenacity
20. Beaver – industrious
21. Gorgon – dreadful and vituperative
22. Fox – cunning
23. Dove/pigeon – peace
24. Ogre – giant
25. Chimera – fantasy

CHAPTER 38

Other Interesting Tidbits

1. It is believed 'E' is the most commonly used letter in any word in English. However, an interesting piece is often shared among English language lovers.

   Reputed Bengali poet and social reformer Ishwar Chandra Vidyasagar asked Michael Madhusudan Dutt, an Anglophile poet if he could make a sentence without using a single 'E'.

   Michael Madhusudan Dutt wrote: "I doubt I can. Its a major part of many words. Omitting it is as hard as making muffins without flour, it's as hard as spitting without saliva, napping without a pillow, driving a train without tracks, sailing to Russia without a boat, washing your hands without soap. And, anyway, what would I gain? An award? A cash bonus? Bragging rights? Why should I strain my brain? It's not worth it."
2. The names of all the continents end with the same letter that they start with.
3. 'Stewardesses' is the longest word typed with only the left hand.
4. 'Typewriter' is the longest word that uses only one row of the Keyboard.
5. RHYTHM is the longest English word without a vowel.
6. The longest word that can be made in the English language using all the letters in alphabetic order is ALMOST.
7. Letter 'B' happens to be the beginning letter of more capital cities than any other.
8. Saying 'GOODBYE'. Have you ever wondered why we say 'goodbye' while parting from our friends or family?

   'Goodbye' happens to be the short form of the Phrase 'God be with you'. Travelling in the middle ages was fraught with danger as roads were bad and infested with robbers. The journey from one place to another was time-consuming and uncertain. Fear of contacting disease on the way too added to the danger of travel. Those undertaking a journey needed the protection that only God could give them. Hence 'God be with you' was uttered during parting which got shortened to 'goodbye' with time.

It is common to utter 'Bless you', when someone sneezes because while a person sneezes his heart stops for a millisecond.

9. 'Sorry' – A common word exchanged between people who feel related. The Old German language inherited it as 'sore' meaning 'pain'. Later in old English it became 'sarig' meaning 'pained' or distressed. It continued with a variant spelling 'sorry'.
10. Orange, month, purple, silver do not have rhyming words in English.
11. Angry and hungry are the only two words in English that end with 'gry'.
12. UNDERGROUND is the only word that begins and ends in UND.
13. DREAMT is the only word that ends in 'MT'
14. Of all the words in English language, the word 'SET' has the most definitions.
15. The number '4' is the only number that has the same number of letters in it - 'FOUR'.
16. The least used letter in the alphabet in English is Q.
17. The most commonly used word in English conversation is 'I'
18. The dot on top of the letter 'i' is called a tittle.
19. The word UNCOPYRIGHTABLE is the only 15 letter word that can be spelled without repeating any letter.
20. There are only 3 sets of letters on a keyboard that are in alphabetical order 'FGH', 'JKL', 'OP'.
21. 'BOOKKEEPER' and 'BOOKKEEPING' are the only words in English with 3 consecutive double letters.
22. The word QUEUE is the only word that is still pronounced the same way when the last 4 letters are removed.
23. The oldest word in English language is TOWN.
24. The past tense of DARE is DURST.

25. STRENGTH is the longest word with one vowel.
26. There are only four words in English that end in 'dous'. Hazardous, horrendous, stupendous, tremendous.
27. The words BEHAVIOUR, EDUCATION, MOZAMBIQUE contain all the 5 vowels of English.
28. One of the funniest words in English is EMPTY. If you remove the 1st letter 'E', you get MPTY. Remove the last letter 'Y', you still get MPT. If you remove the 1st, 3rd and last letters you have MT. Remove all letters you are empty.
29. SUPERCALIFRAGILISTICEXPIALIDOCIOUS – word used to describe something extraordinary.

CHAPTER 39

One to Ten-Letter Words in English

Found this amazing, anonymous piece:

The most damaging one-letter word
I—avoid it

The most satisfying two-letter word
WE—use it

The most poisonous three-letter word
EGO—kill it

The most appreciated four-letter word
LOVE—express it

The most pleasing five-letter word
SMILE—flash it

The fastest spreading six-letter word
RUMOUR—ignore it

The most enviable seven-letter word
SUCCESS—achieve it

The most nefarious eight-letter word
JEALOUSY—leave it

The most powerful nine-letter word
KNOWLEDGE—acquire it

The most essential ten-letter word
CONFIDENCE—trust it

CHAPTER 40

Another Timeless Truth

Time is slow when you wait
Time is fast when you are late
Time is deadly when you are sad
Time is short when you are happy
Time is endless when you are in pain
Time is long when you feel bored
Everytime Time is determined by
Your feelings and situations and not by
A watch
Timepiece or clock!

CHAPTER 41

A Potpourri of Words in English Usage

1. Not quite the same: Luxuriant/Luxurious – Luxuriant refers to rich fertile growth in plants or in hair, feathers or fur while luxurious refers to extremely comfortable, expensive things.
2. Allusion, illusion, delusion
   (a) Allusion is a passing reference to something.
   (b) Illusion is a false impression, temporary
   (c) Delusion is a false illusion fixed in one's mind, accepted as true
3. Alternate, alternative
   (a) Alternate: to occur repeatedly in turns
   (b) Alternative: refers to a choice between two things
4. Prescribe/proscribe
   (a) Prescribe – recommend the use of something.
   (b) Proscribe – to forbid something.
5. Prodigy – an unusually talented child.
   Protege – (pronounced protayzhay) a person helped by a more powerful and influential person.
6. Elicit – to draw forth
   Illicit – unlawful
7. Inflammable – easily set on fire
   Inflammatory – tending to excite
8. Mendacity – habitual lying
   Mendicity – practice of begging
9. Allude – to refer
   Elude – to evade

Other trivia:

1. OK – informal way of saying 'all right'.
2. Participles – forms of the verb which end in '-ing', '-ed', '-n'. They are used to form certain verbs.
3. Present Participle ends in '-ing'—I was cycling downhill.
4. Past Participle ends in '-ed', '-d', '-t', '-n' etc.—He responded, hurt and saddened.
6. Catch 22 – A situation in which a person can't win because one course of action depends on another one, which in turn depends on the first.
7. Caret a mark (/\ ) used for insertion, Cedilla – A mark placed under a letter to show the pronunciation, e.g. in French under a 'Ç' to show it is pronounced 'S' not 'K'. FAÇADE 'fassahd'.
8. Cliché – pronounced 'kleeshay', a word or phrase which was once lively but lost its impact over the years due to overuse.
9. Connoisseur – coneser – an expert who enjoys details of an art or food.
10. Pseudonym – (Syoodonim) a fictitious name used by an author.
11. Questionnaire – Kwestyonare or Kestyonare – A list of questions with a choice of answers for the purpose of survey.
12. Saccharine – pronounced Sakarin – sweet substance used as a sugar substitute.
13. Victuals is pronounced as 'vittles'.
14. Its – belonging to it – My book is not in its usual shelf.
    It's – the abbreviated form of 'it is' – 'It's a lovely day!'
15. Apostrophe – An apostrophe must not be used in the word 'its' when it denotes possession. But one's, other's, either's take the apostrophe e.g. It's its shape that makes it strange.
16. Lieutenant – 'Leftenant' in British English 'Lootenant' in American English.
17. The word having the most synonyms in the Oxford Thesaurus of English is: GOOD with 380 synonyms.
18. The words FISH, TOOTHBRUSH, FRUIT and MILLIONAIRE do not have any synonyms.

Some fun:

(a) What is the difference between a school master and a station master?

One trains the mind while the other minds the train.

(b) What did the detective suspect when he saw peacock feathers? Fowl Play.

(c) Why are goods sent by ship called CARGO and goods sent by truck called SHIPMENT?

(d) Which letter is silent in the word scent, the s or the c?

Chapter 42

Odd Sounding Words you Might Not Know

1. The little toe or finger – minimus
2. The space between the nostrils – Columella nasi
3. The smooth space between the eyebrows – glabella
4. The day after tomorrow is called – overmorrow
5. The pleasant smell accompanying the first rain after a dry spell – petrichor
6. The armhole in garments where the sleeve is sewn – armscye (armsai)
7. Illegible handwriting or scrawl – griffonage
8. The rumbling sound in stomach – wamble
9. The prongs of a fork – tines (i as 'I')
10. The metallic object that measures your boot size at the shoe store – Brannock device
11. A question mark combined with an exclamatory mark (?!) – interrobang
12. Difficulty in getting out of bed in the morning after waking up – dysania (disania)
13. The sick feeling after overeating or drinking – crapulence
14. The plastic or metallic coating at the tip of the shoelace – aglet
15. The luminous swirls or stars you see when closing your eyes tight by pressing them with your hands – phosphenes
16. The meaningless lyrics of la, la, la or na, na, na in a song – vocables

Chapter 43

Contracted Forms of Modal Verbs and Question Tags

When people converse with one another, they do not pronounce every word distinctly. They tend to join two words and omit vowels and consonants.

Contracted forms of modal verbs can be seen as:

1. do + not = don't
2. did + not = didn't
3. is + not = isn't
4. are + not = aren't
5. can + not = can't
6. could + not = couldn't
7. must + not = mustn't
8. need + not = needn't
9. should + not = shouldn't
10. would + not = wouldn't
11. has + not = hasn't
12. have + not = haven't

But what is the contracted form of will + not = ? It is won't

Shall + not = shan't.

Confusing? Is it?

Often found in question tags, the contracted forms of modal verbs are widely used in common speech. Question tags are nothing but short questions at the end of a statement. A positive or affirmative statement takes on a negative tag while a negative statement takes on a positive tag that ends in a question mark.

Affirmative statements, negative tags.

1. It is a beautiful day.
   It is a beautiful day, isn't it?
2. My little brother can go out to play.
   My little brother can go out to play, can't he?
3. They will certainly come to meet me here tomorrow.
   They will certainly come to meet me here tomorrow, won't they?

Negative statements, positive tags.

1. We must not get wet in the rain.
   We must not get wet in the rain, must we?
2. He does not have basic manners.
   He does not have basic manners, does he?
3. The baby can not talk clearly.
   The baby can not talk clearly, can he?

Imperative sentences expressing orders, requests, suggestions, tend to take on either an affirmative or negative tag.eg.

1. Switch off the light.
   Switch off the light, will you?
2. Fetch me the newspaper.
   Fetch me the newspaper, won't you?
3. Hand me the scissors.
   Hand me the scissors, will you, please?
   Hand me the scissors, would you?
4. Please wait for me.
   Please wait for me, won't you?
5. Let's go out for a walk.
   Let's go out for a walk, shall we?

CHAPTER 44

Some Common Literary Terms

1. Allegory – In an allegory, there is a fixed and coherent system of signs whereas a symbol can stand alone, serve a temporary purpose, a flash of illumination. A story that has a hidden theme. Eg. Orwell's 'Animal Farm'.
2. Symbolism is not the same as Allegory. It is a literary device using words, objects, ideas as symbols.
3. Romanticism – Artistic movement that directly or unrestrainedly expresses or seeks to source personal emotion; anti-classicism.
4. Romance – Pleasing and idealized love story; non-realistic fiction; fiction with a mysterious charm or sentimental atmosphere.
5. Realism – Attempt to describe in literature some fact as it actually is especially in its unpleasant aspect.
6. Realist – One who claims to be without illusions.
7. Classical – Literature in accordance with accepted tastes and traditions; of recognized merit, restrained, austere and balanced.
8. Parable – Short story with the hidden moral or spiritual meaning.
9. Transcendentalism – Mysticism, philosophy that believes spirituality can be achieved through self-reflection. Union of social with divine, or individualism, idealism and the divinity of nature.
10. Euphemism – Pronounced Yoofemism—a milder, more amusing word to replace the usual term for an unpleasant, tragic or embarrassing thing.
11. Limerick – A humorous poem of five lines.
12. Ode – A poem or song in irregular lyric form.
13. Wit – Power of imagination.
14. Humor – The ability to perceive something amusing; comical.

15. Diction – Choice of words, manner of speaking.
16. Syntax – The rules for arranging or combining words in sentences.
17. Anagram – A word which forms another word if the letters are rearranged.
18. Rebus – A puzzle combining a letter with a picture to form a word.
19. Aphorism – It is a concise statement of general truth. Almost similar to an adage, maxim or proverb, an Aphorism is often used to teach a lesson or focus on moral instruction. For instance:
    (a) Absence makes the heart fonder.
    (b) Its nice to be important but important to be nice.
    (c) No success is final, no failure is fatal.
20. Ambivalence – Coexistence of two opposite emotions, especially love and hate towards the same object.
21. Asyndeton – The absence of a conjunction between parts of a sentence e.g. I came, I saw, I conquered.
22. Anticlimax – Weak ending; sudden descent to the ridiculous.
23. Aphthong – Letter in word not sounded (as b in debt).
24. Archaic – Out of date.

CHAPTER 45

Fascinating English, Indeed!

Some parts of the body are used either as verbs in the physical sense or as metaphors.

1. If you acquire a job forcefully, you **muscle** your way into it. If you want to **elbow** out someone from the work place, you use **arm** tactics.
2. You may **head** an organization but be prepared to **shoulder** the blame if things go awry or else you will **face** the music.
3. A responsible boss will **back** his office staff. But if the members don't **toe** the line, the topmost executive can **skin** them.
4. You may **eye** someone with suspicion but the detective will **finger** the suspicion.
5. Just **hand** over all the papers to me. I will **thumb** a ride and rush to the office.
6. During the program, the children **mouth** the songs on the stage with confidence.
7. I can't **stomach** the idea of staying indoors all day.
8. My friend loves to **foot** the bill after dinner.

Chapter 46

Words that Fit into these Meanings or One-Word Substitutes

1. Talking in one's sleep – Somniloquence
2. The art of paper folding – Origami
3. Collecting of postage stamps – Philately
4. Goods thrown overboard to lighten a ship – Jetsam
5. The class of mammals that carry their young in a pouch – Marsupials
6. The rearing of silkworms for producing raw silk – Sericulture
7. Living both on land and water – Amphibious
8. Wreckage found floating on the surface of the sea – Flotsam
9. The study of coins – Numismatics
10. Fortune-telling by means of playing cards – Cartomancy
11. A case for holding arrows – Quiver
12. An exaggerated statement not to be taken literally – Hyperbole
13. A legendary animal with body of a lion and head and wings of an eagle – Griffin
14. The science of projectiles – Ballistics
15. A two-hundredth anniversary – Bicentenary
16. The nesting place of a swarm of bees – Honeycomb
17. The smallest pig of a litter – Tantony

18. A rain water spout in the form of a grotesque human or animal head – Gargoyle
19. A word or sentence that reads the same backwards and forwards – Palindrome
20. A device intended to aid the memory – Mnemonic
21. A group of six persons or things – Sextet
22. The killing of one's own brother – Fratricide
23. The killing of self – Suicide
24. The killing of one's sister – Sororicide
25. The killing of one's mother – Matricide
26. The killing of one's father – Patricide
27. The killing of one's wife – Uxoricide
28. The killing of a king – Regicide
29. The killing of a Priest/Prophet – Vaticide
30. The killing of God – Deicide
31. The killing of babies – Infanticide
32. The killing of unborn babies – Foeticide
33. The illegal killing of a person by another – Homicide
34. The killing of a race of people – Genocide
35. The killing of insects or pests – Pesticide
36. A pair of eyeglasses with a spring which clips the nose – Pince-nez
37. A small lizard that can change its color – Chameleon
38. One who specializes in caves or cave systems – Speleologist
39. A person who worships one God – Monotheist
40. A person who doesn't believe in God – Atheist
41. A person who is not sure of the existence of god – Agnostic
42. A person speaking or writing several languages – Polyglot
43. The practice of a woman having many husbands – Polyandry

44. The study of handwriting especially for character analysis – Graphology
45. A person who draws or produces maps – Cartographer
46. A person who compiles dictionaries – Lexicographer
47. An unofficial title given to somebody or something – Sobriquet
48. Some Sobriquets:
    (a) The man of destiny – Napolean
    (b) The lion of Judah – David
    (c) The Ebony antelope – Jesse Owens
    (d) The lion of Punjab – Ranjit Singh
    (e) The firebrand of India – Aurobindo Ghosh
    (f) Little Corporal – Napoleon
    (g) The maid of Orleans – Joan of Arc
    (h) The Black Pearl – Pele
    (i) The lady with the lamp – Florence Nightingale
    (j) The light of Asia – Gautama Buddha
    (k) The Bard of Avon – William Shakespeare
    (l) The eternal city – Rome
49. Anything that cannot be burnt is said to be incombustible
50. Anything that cannot be called back is said to be irrevocable
51. Anything that cannot be corrected is said to be incorrigible
52. Anything that cannot be conquered is said to be invincible
53. Anything that cannot be heard is said to be inaudible
54. Anything that cannot be moved by entreaty is said to be inexorable
55. Anything that cannot be read is said to be illegible
56. Anything that cannot be imitated is said to be inimitable
57. Anything that cannot be satisfied is said to be insatiable
58. Anything that cannot be dissolved is said to be insoluble
59. Those who eat grains are called graminivorous

60. Those who eat herbs are called herbivorous
61. Those who eat fruits are called frugivorous
62. Those who eat flesh are called carnivorous
63. Those who eat insects are called insectivorous
64. Those who eat fish are called piscivorous
65. Those who eat everything are called omnivorous
66. Those who eat vegetables are called vegetarians
67. Those who take vegetarian food without dairy products like cheese and milk are called vegans
68. Those who eat human flesh are called cannibals
69. Those animals that naturally prey on other animals are called predators
70. Things which happen once in a year – annual
71. Things which happen once in two years – biennial
72. Things which happen once in three years – triennial
73. Things which happen once in four years – quadriennial
74. Things which happen once in five years – quinquennial
75. Things which happen once in six years – sexennial
76. Things which happen once in seven years – septennial
77. Things which happen once in eight years – octennial
78. Things which happen once in nine years – novennial
79. Things which happen once in ten years – decennial
80. Things which happen once in twenty years – vicennial
81. Things which happen once in hundred years – centennial
82. Things which happen once in thousand years – millennial
83. One who hates mankind is called misanthrope
84. One who hates women is called misogynist
85. One who hates marriage is called misogamist
86. One who hates god is called misotheist
87. One who hates knowledge is called misologist
88. One who loves mankind is called philanthropist
89. One who loves women is called philogynist
90. One who loves books is called bibliophile
91. One who knows everything is called omniscient

92. One who is all powerful is called omnipotent
93. One who is present everywhere is called omnipresent
94. One who has universal knowledge is called pantologic
95. A man who is liked by the people is called popular
96. A man who is well known for his goodness is called famous
97. A man who has an evil reputation is called notorious
98. A man who looks to the bright side of things is called an optimist
99. A man who looks to the dark side of things is called a pessimist
100. A man who regards the whole world as his own home or regards himself as a citizen of the world is called a cosmopolite
101. A man who is skilled in many languages is called a linguist
102. A man who is partner subordinate in a crime is called an accomplice
103. A man who respects old traditions is called orthodox
104. A man who believes that pleasure is the chief good of life is called a hedonist
105. A man who indulges in boastful talk is called a braggart
106. A man who always thinks of himself is called an egoist
107. A man who denies all existing doctrines is called a nihilist
108. A man who can use both hands with equal skills is called ambidextrous
109. A man who dies for one's country is called a martyr
110. A man who rides on horseback is called an equestrian
111. A man who walks on foot is called a pedestrian
112. A man who believes in fate is called a fatalist
113. A man who has regards for others is called altruist
114. A man who is disposed to weeping is called lachrymose
115. A man who makes a display of his learning is called pedant
116. A man who is subject to death is called mortal
117. A man who is deathless is called immortal
118. A man who speaks two languages is called bilinguist
119. A man who speaks many languages is called multilinguist
120. A person who is sixty years old is called a sexagenarian
121. A person who is seventy years old is called septuagenarian

122. A person who is eighty years old is called an octogenarian
123. A person who is ninety odd years is called a nonagenarian
124. A person who is hundred years old is called a centenarian
125. A person who is very fond of refined sensuous enjoyment is called an epicure
126. A person who thinks of welfare of women is called a feminist
127. A person who dies without making a will is called an intestate
128. A person who walks while fast asleep is called somnambulist
129. A person who talks while fast asleep is called a somnilquist
130. A person who is indifferent to pleasure or pain is called a stoic
131. A person who always thinks that he is ill is called a valetudinarian
132. Anything through which one can see is called transparent
133. Anything through which one can only dimly see is called translucent
134. Anything through which one cannot see at all is called opaque
135. The life of a person is called biography
136. The life of a person written by himself is called autobiography
137. A book published after the death of its author is called posthumous
138. A two-footed animal is called biped
139. A four-footed animal is called quadruped
140. A hundred-footed insect is called centipede
141. A remedy for all diseases is called panacea
142. The style using too many words is called verbose
143. The use of a delicate word in place of an offensive one is called euphemism
144. A thing producing opposite result is called an antidote
145. Disease caused by touch is called contagious; disease spread through air is called infectious
146. Disease to which many men or people are a prey is called an epidemic
147. A disease peculiar to a country is called an endemic; a disease that spreads over an entire country or the whole world is called a Pandemic

148. The act of stealing the writing of other people and passing it as one's own is called plagiarism
149. To insert passages in an author's work or to fill up gaps in a series is called interpolate
150. A building where dead people are kept is called mortuary
151. To establish justice of a cause is called vindicate
152. Bent on revenge, inspired by resentment is called vindictive
153. The science of deciphering ancient manuscripts or impressions is called Palaeography
154. The art of engraving on wood is known as Xylography
155. The study of correct pronunciation of words of a language is Orthoepy
156. The communication from one person to another without the use of normal sense organs is Telepathy
157. The ability to speak a language without having learnt it is known as Xenoglossy
158. A person with a bad handwriting or spelling is called a cacographic person
159. The science and art of teaching is referred to as Pedagogy
160. The art of trimming trees into ornamental shapes is Topiary
161. The art, study or process of engraving gems is Glyptography
162. Physical geography dealing with formation of mountains is Orography
163. A word made of the initial letters of an official title etc. is an Acronym
164. The offspring of a whale, moose, seal, elephant or hippopotamus is called a calf
165. The female of a hare, deer, antelope or kangaroo is known as a doe
166. The study of population statistics is called demography
167. The art of curing and stuffing animal skins is known as Taxidermy
168. The performance of an artist on stage where he creates the illusion as if his voice is coming from a puppet is called Ventriloquy.

CHAPTER 47

Idioms and Phrases

Idiom—A group of words that has a particular meaning, quite different from the usual meaning of words used separately. It also means a language that is natural to a speaker.

1. To take with a grain of salt – To be cautious.
2. To hit below the belt – To take undue and mean advantage of.
3. To steal a march – To excel in progress.
4. Broken reed – A person not worthy of trust.
5. Topsy Turvy – Upside down.
6. To beggar description – Beyond description.
7. To bring down the house – To impress the audience.
8. A queer fish – A strange fellow.
9. To cry hoarse – To shout to the extent of affecting one's throat.
10. To be a hard nut to crack – Something very difficult to do.
11. To add insult to injury – First to injure a person and then to insult him, so indicating a second act against a person.
12. Alive and kicking – Active and full of energy, especially with reference to somebody who has been inactive, out of the running perhaps ill.
13. That's all moonshine – That's all rubbish; I do not believe a word of it.
14. All the rage – (something) That suddenly comes into great, but usually temporary fashion.
15. Alma mater – University, college, school, where one was educated.
16. Alpha and Omega – A rather pretentious alternative for first and last, beginning and end.

17. An arm-chair critic – A person who irresponsibly passes criticisms, especially unfavorable, on something of which he has no first-hand, practical, knowledge.
18. To bring home the bacon – To succeed in an undertaking, to provide material support.
19. A Baker's Dozen – Thirteen
20. The be-all and end-all – The essential aim with the accomplishment of which the affair ends.
21. To bell the cat – To undertake for the common good a dangerous task that will make an enemy harmless; or, to undertake the dangerous part in a course of action.
22. The benefit of the doubt – The assumption, when there are two possible alternatives, and proof is not possible, that a person is not culpable or guilty.
23. To be too big for his boots – To consider himself too important for his present position and occupation.
24. A bitter pill – An unpleasant, especially a disappointing blow that one has to endure.
25. As black as thunder – The expression always refers to the facial expression of a person who looks violently angry.
26. To blaze a trail – To initiate preparatory work in a movement, cause, etc
27. As bold as brass – Extremely or excessively bold or impudent.
28. To buttonhole a person – To go up to a person and engage his attention on some matter, unexpectedly
29. To jump from the frying pan into the fire – To escape from a bad situation to get into a worse one instead.
30. The cat among the pigeons – The 'cat' here refers to a dangerous, powerful, person who will victimize a number of people incapable of making resistance.
31. As cheap as dirt – Extremely cheap and worthless.
32. To claim one's pound of flesh – To insist on one's rights and ruthlessly exact payment or service, even when that means extreme hardship.

33. To be in the clouds – A person, day-dreaming, whose mind is filled with visionary thoughts.
34. Under a cloud – In disfavor, in disrepute, under suspicion, with a slur on one's character.
35. To cook a person's goose – To ruin him. To ruin a particular project etc.
36. What's cooking? – What's happening? What mischief is brewing? What are you up to?
37. To have the courage of one's convictions – To have the courage to speak or to act in accordance with what one believes in.
38. Crestfallen – Dejected, abashed.
39. To crow over – To exult excitedly or conceitedly about one's success.
40. To cry for the moon – To want, set one's heart on something that is impossible to get.
41. To talk shop – To speak exclusively about one's business or profession.
42. To turn the corner – To pass the crisis.
43. To go against the grain – To be distasteful or contrary to one's principle.
44. To wash one's hands of – To be relieved of.
45. Geese or swans – Praise of one's things.
46. A man of many parts – A man with great talent in different areas.
47. To pull the wool over somebody's eyes – To deceive.
48. To spin a yarn – To repeat something.
49. Moonshine – Bright happy days.
50. To pay off old scores – Compensate an old account.
51. To be under the fog – To be in cloudy and doubtful condition.
52. To go through fire and water – To face many hardships.
53. To pay through the nose – To pay a very high price.
54. All and sundry – Everybody without distinction.
55. Swan song – Last and pathetic song before death.

56. Scot free – Without punishment.
57. Stuff and nonsense – Foolish talks.
58. Smooth sailing – In a smooth way.
59. To be on one's guard – To be vigilant.
60. To nip in the bud – To curb evil in its initial stages of growth.
61. To play the game – To be serious about something.
62. To let the cat out of the bag – To allow the secret to be leaked.
63. To bring home to – To make known to.
64. To talk tall – To boast.
65. To be down and out – Extremely tired.
66. To be an ugly customer – A troublesome person.
67. Close shave – Narrow escape.
68. To fall flat – To fail.
69. An uphill task – Difficult problem.
70. To go to the dogs – To suffer.
71. To cut the ground under a person's feet – To throw him in an undertaking etc, to make his position untenable.
72. To cut no ice – To make no impression, to have no effect.
73. To look, to speak daggers – To look at, to speak to a person with hostility, i.e. with glances or words that pierce like a dagger.
74. To dance attendance on a person – To be constantly in his company, paying attention to his every wish and whim.
75. To die in harness – To die while still actively engaged in the course of one's regular work.
76. A Don Juan – Sexually loose man of the upper classes, the proverbial seducer.
77. A doubting Thomas – A person who, in a particular matter, or in general by temperament, is noted for his incredulity.
78. An El Dorado – A country of great wealth, or loose source where a fortune can be made.
79. To fight like Kilkenny cats – To fight fiercely.
80. A queer fish – A strange or mysterious person.
81. As fit as a fiddle – In a first-rate physical condition.

82. To fly off the handle – To lose one's temper.
83. A fool's Paradise – A state of illusory happiness and prosperity that will later be shown to have been unreal and will be shattered.
84. A Frankenstein – A monster created by Mary Shelly in the novel Frankenstein. It refers to a person who falls a victim to his own creation.
85. The gift of the gab – Facility in speaking.
86. Give him an inch and he will take an ell – A person who, if, given any concession will take advantage by making further demands.
87. To give a person a piece of one's mind – To tell him in strong terms one's unfavorable opinion of his conduct or character.
88. To go to seed – Of people, to be past one's prime, to deteriorate, to degenerate, to become useless.
89. A good Samaritan – A kind hearted charitable person who goes to help those in need, even if they are strangers.
90. To grease a person's palm – To bribe a person with money in order to extract service, information, etc.
91. A hang-dog look – An appearance of guilt combined with depression or being ashamed of oneself.
92. Don't judge a book by its cover – You should not judge or evaluate a person just by his or her outward appearance.
93. Hare-brained – A person with disconnected, wild thoughts.
94. To cool one's heels – Originally and literally, to rest after walking.
95. To hum and haw – To speak hesitatingly, with inarticulate sounds between words, phrases, clauses, sentences.
96. To have a hunch – To have a suspicion, intuition, premonition.
97. A hurly-burly – A commotion, an uproar, confusion, strife.
98. Out of joint – In a state of disorder, disorganization, disharmony, corruption.
99. To keep at arm's length – To avoid close relations with a person.
100. A labour of love – Work undertaken solely or chiefly from interest in it, or form affection for a person for whom it is done, and not for the remuneration, credit, etc., gained.

101. To leave a door open – To arrange matters such that a compromise or agreement is possible.
102. Like a bull in a China shop – Extremely clumsy, blundering, troublesome.
103. Like a house on fire – Extremely quickly or easily, and often to one's great satisfaction.
104. Molly-coddle – Pamper a child or adult or treat him with excessive care.
105. To be monarch of all one surveys – To be in a situation of triumphant and unquestioned mastery.
106. A nail in one's coffin – Something that will shorten one's life, or sometimes, will ruin one's career or one's plan.
107. To look for a needle in a haystack (or in a bottle of hay) – To search for one small thing in a space so wide or among such a multitude of things that it is almost hopeless to find it.
108. Nom de plume – Fictitious name under which an author writes.
109. To bite off a person's nose – To speak sharply to him.
110. To turn up one's nose at – To regard a person or thing with contempt.
111. To the nth degree – To any degree or number or extent.
112. Null and void – Having no legal force, invalid, inoperative.
113. In a nutshell – Put concisely.
114. Off and on – At intervals; with interruption and resumption of action.
115. An open secret – a piece of information that, though formally supposed to be a secret, is a matter of general information.
116. To feather one's nest – To give material benefits to the people of one's own family.
117. French leave – Absence without permission.
118. To carry all before one – To impress the gathering.
119. To keep body and soul together – To maintain oneself with dignity.
120. To smell a rat – To suspect something.

121. To be an upstart – To get a sudden rise of fortune.
122. To dance to the tune – To go by the guidance of.
123. To pick up the gauntlet –To accept a challenge.
124. To keep up appearances – To maintain outward prestige.
125. To rack one's brain – To think deeply.
126. To come to grief – To suffer.
127. Hush money – Bribe.
128. To stick to one's guns – To be firm to one's stand.
129. Wet blanket – Discouraging or weeping fellow.
130. To cross the rubicon – To cross initial hurdles.
131. Dutch courage – Courage executed by wine.
132. Helter skelter – In a state of confusion.
133. To blow hot and cold in the same breath – To oscillate.
134. A cock and bull story – A concocted story.
135. Green horn – An inexperienced person.
136. To worship the rising sun – To obey the authority in power.
137. To be an eyesore – To be unpleasant.
138. To let the sleeping dogs lie – Not to disturb the troublesome person.
139. To have a windfall – To have a sudden fortune.
140. To carry fire and sword – To go on a rampage to destroy the enemy.
141. To cut no ice – To produce no effect.
142. To pinch the belly – To cut one's expenses to bear minimum needs.
143. To be on the razor's edge – To be exposed to danger.
144. To be henpecked – Husband under the domination of his wife.
145. To put the Thames on fire – To do something impossible.
146. To bury the hatchet – To forget old enmity.
147. To get into a mess – To get confused.
148. To give the devil his due – To recognize the good points in a bad person.

149. A coquette's smile – A clever devise to dupe.
150. To be in one's element – To be in a congenial or comfortable position.
151. Fair and square – Straightforward.
152. Palmy days – Prosperous days.
153. To be lice in the hair – To be spread all round.
154. To be cast down – To be depressed.
155. To be the brick and mortar of – To be the solid foundation of.
156. To paint the town red – To have a riotously gay time.
157. Part and parcel – A necessary, essential element in an arrangement etc.
158. A man of parts – A man of capacity, talents, intellectual ability.
159. Penny-wise and pound-foolish – Careful in spending money on things that cost a little, but wasteful when it comes to those that cost a lot.
160. Petticoat government – Excessive rule of women in the home, or excessive influence by them in politics.
161. The pick of the bunch – The best of a set of people or things.
162. From pillar to post – Physically, from one place to another.
163. Piping hot – Extremely hot.
164. To play with fire – To trifle with danger; to engage lightly in an affair that has dangers in it and may lead to disastrous results.
165. To plume oneself – To pride oneself.
166. To pocket one's pride – To consent to do something, or to endure having something said or done to one without resistance or protest.
167. Post-haste – With all possible speed.
168. To pull up a person – To interrupt or rebuke a person in the course of his conduct or language.
169. To draw or pull the wool over a person's eyes – To deceive somebody.
170. A lame duck – An incompetent, useless person.

171. To put the best foot (or leg) forward – To work as fast as one can, to make as energetic efforts as one can to do things quickly.
172. To put on one's thinking cap – To give serious consideration to a matter.
173. The three R's – Reading, (w)riting, (a)rithmetic, regarding as the necessary fundamental subjects of primary education.
174. The rank and file – Militarily this is used to mean the body of private soldiers and non-commissioned officers.
175. A rap on the knuckles – A sharp rebuke for a fault.
176. To read between the lines – To find a meaning or purpose not obvious or explicitly expressed in something written, or spoken or done.
177. A red-letter day – An important and memorable day.
178. To rise like the Phoenix – To rise with new life and vigour from the remains of what is dead or obsolete.
179. To rub shoulders – To be in close contact or on informal terms with someone.
180. In one's salad days – In the time of one's youthful experience.
181. The salt of the earth – The finest type of humanity.
182. A saving grace – A redeeming virtue.
183. To sell like hot cakes – To have a big and quick sale.
184. Sermons in stones – Morals, lessons, truths, that can be learnt from natural things.
185. An open sesame – An immediate and infallible way of dealing with a particular problem.
186. Afraid of his own shadow – Subject to groundless and trivial fears.
187. To step into a person's shoes – By promotion or otherwise to occupy the position another person had, in employment, reputation, etc.
188. A sine qua non – An essential, a necessity, an indispensable thing or person.
189. More sinned against than sinning – More wronged and injured by, than doing wrong and injury to others.

190. To dress to the nines – To wear fashionable attire for a special occasion.
191. To speak volumes – To reveal a great deal in extremely few words; without saying a word, by a gesture or look.
192. To spill the beans – To let out a secret.
193. The spirit is willing, but the flesh is weak – One's higher impulse is conquered by the weakness in human nature.
194. A stick-in-the-mud – A person without enterprise, initiative, adventure, who runs in a groove or is in a rut.
195. To stir up a hornet's nest – By indiscreet action especially interference, to rouse violent opposition among people that involves one in serious trouble.
196. A storm in a tea-cup – Disturbance, fuss, excited concern, over a trifling matter.
197. A strait jacket; strait waistcoat – A garment of strong material, able to be tightly laced, used for the restraint of violent prisoners.
198. With his tail between his legs – Showing dejection or admission of defeat, like a whipped dog cringing.
199. A walk-over – An extremely easy win.
200. A white lie – An untruth that is regarded as forgivable, not serious; or harmless; or sometimes even, when the motive is to comfort or otherwise benefit.
201. Widow's weeds – Black mourning clothes worn by a widow.
202. Wishful thinking – Letting oneself believe, indulging in the belief, that what you would like to be true is true.
203. To throw in the towel – To give up or stop doing something having realized you can't succeed.
204. Yeomen's service – An excellent service.
205. To move heaven and earth – To make one's utmost efforts.
206. Sour grapes – Something that cannot be achieved.
207. Tots and pots – Domestic worries.
208. Through thick and thin – Through all obstacles and difficulties.
209. Toil and moil – Labor.

210. Tooth and nail – Vehemently with all power.
211. Under a cloud – Disfavor.
212. Weal or woe – Happiness or misery.
213. Wear and tear – Wastage or damage caused by overuse of objects.
214. White elephant – A profession which proves to be burdensome.
215. White livered – Coward.
216. Wet bargain – Agreement made while drinking.
217. White flag – Surrender to the enemy.
218. To be underway – To make progress.
219. To be in hot water – To be in trouble or difficulty.
220. To break the ice – To get through the first difficulty.
221. To burn the candle at both ends – To use up extravagantly.
222. To burn one's fingers – To get into trouble.
223. To break a butterfly on the wheel – To waste power.
224. To burn the midnight oil – To work late at night.
225. To bite one's lips – To control anger.
226. To bell the cat – To take leading part of any hazardous movement.
227. To beat black and blue – To beat till one's body is discoloured.
228. To be on the carpet – To be under consideration or discussion.
229. To cross t's and dot i's – To make minor change.
230. To call a spade a spade – To speak the plain truth.
231. To cast oil on troubled waters – To make the situation calm.
232. To count the chickens before they are hatched – To anticipate gains on leisure basis.
233. To cry for the moon – To hope for an impossible thing.
234. To curl one's lips – To be angry.
235. To cry over spilt milk – To waste time in useless regret.
236. To end in smoke – To fail totally.
237. To fly kites – To spread rumours.
238. To fly doves – To lead a happy life.
239. To be footloose and fancy free – Having no romantic attachments.
240. To go to the dogs – To be ruined.

241. To get on one's nerves - To irritate one.
242. To give quarters – To be merciful.
243. To go to the wall – To be unsuccessful.
244. To give cold shoulder to someone – To show indifference.
245. To have too many irons in the fire – To be engaged or financially interested in too many enterprises.
246. To have a bee in one's bonnet – To be crazy in a certain direction.
247. To have a finger in the pie – To take active part in something.
248. To leap in the dark – To act without thinking over the result.
249. To lead to the altar – To marry.
250. To lay by the heels – To imprison.
251. To make both ends meet – To live within one's income.
252. To make a clean breast of – The confess fully.
253. To sail before the wind – To be prosperous.
254. To take the tide at the flood – To take advantage of an opportunity.
255. To throw cold water upon – To discourage.
256. To turn on one's little finger – To have complete control over a person.
257. Tip of the iceberg – Just an insignificant thing.
258. To put the cat among the pigeons – To introduce an element of controversy into an argument in order to confuse the issue.
259. To walk the talk – To do what you promise to do; to practice what you preach.
260. A cut above the rest – Better than other people, superior to.
261. Cakes and ale – carefree or easy living.

CHAPTER 48

Proverbs

1. A rolling stone gathers no moss – An unsteady man never succeeds in earning wealth or reputation.
2. All that glitters is not gold – Appearances are often deceptive.
3. A hedge between keeps the friendship green – Just as a hedge between two farms imparts some greenery to lands, in the same way slight aloofness between two friends keeps their friendship fresh and constant.
4. A sleeping fox catches no poultry – An idle man does not get anything.
5. All his geese are swans – A man who always represents his own possessions as better than similar things belonging to another.
6. A wolf in sheep's clothing – A dangerous person who pretends to be quite harmless.
7. As you make your bed so you must lie – You must accept and bear the consequences of your own doings.
8. Blow hot and cold with the same breath – To appear both to favour and to oppose.
9. Blood is thicker than water – Kinship is stronger than friendship.
10. Cut off one's nose to spite one's face – To act from anger in such a way as to injure oneself.
11. Carry coal to Newcastle – To take something where it is already plentiful.
12. Drowning man clutches at a straw – A desperate person will try to use anything for help.
13. Empty vessels make much noise – A man of no worth brags most.
14. Every bullet has its billet – Nothing occurs by chance or is done without some purpose or effect.

15. Every dog has its day – The period of enjoyment allowed to any creature is a short one.
16. Easy come, easy go – What is acquired without effort is spent without thought.
17. Example is better than precept – Action is better than teaching.
18. Every dark cloud has a silver lining – The darkest prospect has some redeeming brightness, nothing wholly dark.
19. Give the devil his due – Do full justice to a person or cause.
20. Let not the pot call the kettle black – Do not criticize your neighbors unless you are free from blame yourself.
21. Make hay while the sun shines – Do not lose an opportunity when it comes.
22. My cake is dough – I am quite disappointed.
23. New brooms sweep clean – Those newly appointed to office are apt to make great changes.
24. One swallow does not make a summer – We must not frame a general law on one single phenomenon.
25. Once bitten twice shy – If the doing of a thing has hurt once it shall not readily be done the next time.
26. Prevention is better than cure – It is better to prevent a misfortune than to find a remedy for it after it has taken place.
27. Proof of the pudding is in the eating – Nothing can be said to be good unless tried.
28. Penny wise and pound foolish – Careful about small profits and foolishly blind to larger and more important gains.
29. Rome was not built in a day – Great things require time and trouble and must not be done hastily.
30. Strike the iron when it is hot – Take the advantage of an opportunity when it arises.
31. Still waters run deep – Wise people are not talkative.
32. There are wheels within wheels – A complication of circumstances.
33. There is no smoke without fire – There is no effect without a cause.
34. The game is not worth the candle – The advantage or enjoyment to be gained is not worth the trouble spent in gaining it.

35. To take the hind-leg off the donkey – To continue to talk and talk without giving up.
36. Donkey's years – For a very long time.
37. To dish out (something) – Give away a lot of compliments, gifts, etc.
38. Dish it out – Attack fiercely (with words, blows etc.,) e.g. don't pick a quarrel with that guy, he can really dish it out.
39. Dish the dirt – Say or spread scandalous things about someone.
40. Fortune favours the brave/the bold – A person who is willing to take risks boldly is often successful.
41. Knowledge is power – A man acquiring knowledge can achieve name and fame and benefit from it.
42. Honesty is the best policy – Being sincere and honest bestows contentment and tranquility in a person.
43. The child is father of the man – Since manhood grows out of childhood the origin of man is a child – a seeming contradiction by William Wordsworth.
44. Sweet are the uses of adversity – Adverse situations teach us tolerance and fortitude which are useful to face challenges in life.
45. A stitch in time saves nine – Timely action can save a lot of extra work later.
46. The hand that rocks the cradle rules the world – The mother grooms and nurtures the infant and molds his character for the future.
47. Familiarity breeds contempt – Getting too close to someone may lead to loss of respect.
48. The grass is always greener on the other side of the fence – It appears other people are in a better situation than you.
49. Those who live in glass houses should not throw stones at others – It is not right to criticize somebody for the faults one possesses.
50. If winter comes, can spring be far behind? – Cold and adverse conditions symbolic of winter are bound to be followed by pleasant and favorable days of spring.

51. To err is human; to forgive, divine – It is common for people to make mistakes but to forgive them is a godly act.
52. A thing of beauty is a joy forever – A beautiful object is always a source of happiness to a person.
53. Fame is the last infirmity of a noble mind – The desire for fame is the last weakness in a person and remains with him till the end of his life.
54. Where there is a will, there is a way – If we have strong determination to do something we will automatically find a way to do it.
55. Experience is the best teacher – We learn from our own experiences and become stronger and wiser in life.

CHAPTER 49

Conditionals

A conditional sentence, often consisting of a main clause and a subordinate clause tells that an action will be performed if a certain condition is fulfilled. Words like if, even if, unless, suppose etc. are used to introduce the condition. There are 3 types of conditional clauses:

Type I: Open or possible condition

There is a possibility that the 'if' event might take place and it has a reference to the future.

Structure: If+verb (simple present): main clause verb (future)

Type II: Hypothetical or unlikely condition

The 'if' event may be hypothetical or unlikely and it may refer to the present or future.

Structure: If + verb (past tense): main clause verb (would/could/might +verb)

Type III: Unfulfilled or did not happen condition

This type of condition refers to the past.

Structure: If + past perfect: main clause verb (would/might/could + verb in perfect form).

Examples of:

- Type I, Open condition – If it rains, I shall stay indoors.
- Type II, Unlikely condition – If it rained, I would stay indoors.
- Type III, Unfulfilled condition – If it had rained, I would have stayed indoors.

Type I: If you work hard you will get a good rank.
Type II: If you worked hard you would get a good rank.
Type III: If you had worked hard you would have got a good rank.

Keeping the structure of the 3 conditionals in mind, it is easy to fit in one half of the sentence after reading the main or subordinate clause that is given. For instance:

1. The function will begin if the chief guest arrives. – Type I Open condition.
2. The function would begin if the chief guest arrived. – Type II Hypothetical condition.
3. The function would have begun if the chief guest had arrived. – Type III unfulfilled condition.

Chapter 50

Important Figures of Speech

Figures of speech are used in literature for producing an emphatic literary effect.

1. Figures based on sounds:

   These are mainly (a) Onomatopoeia (b) Alliteration (c) Pun

   (a) ***Onomatopoeia:*** In this figure the sound of the words is made to echo or suggest the sense. e.g.

      i. Birds twitter.

      ii. Rend with tremendous sound your ears asunder.

      iii. With gun, drum, trumpet, blunderbuss and thunder.

   (b) ***Alliteration:*** Some letter or syllable is repeated at the beginning of two or more words in a sentence. e.g.

      i. The fair breeze blew.

      ii. The fair foam flew.

      iii. The furrow followed free.

   (c) ***Pun:*** This figure of speech consists in a duplicity of sense though there is unity of sound. e.g.

      i. They went and told the sexton, the sexton tolled the bell.

      ii. Not on thy sole, but on thy soul, harsh Jew, thou makest thy knife keen.

   Usually 'Pun' is used to provoke laughter.

2. Figures based on resemblance:

   (a) Simile, (b) Metaphor, (c) Fable (d) Allegory

   (a) ***Simile:*** A Simile consists in formally and clearly expressing likeness existing between two different things. e.g.

      i. As idle as a painted ship upon a painted ocean

      ii. Red as a rose is she.

(b) ***Metaphor:*** A Metaphor is an implied simile e.g.

i. Variety is the spice of life (unclearly stated).

ii. You are the salt of the earth.

iii. Confidence is a plant of slow growth in an aged bosom.

iv. Youth is the seed time of life.

v. She has a fluent tongue.

Here in the above examples the attribute which properly belongs to one object is transferred to another by way of comparison. This comparison is implied but not clearly stated in order to produce a vivid description.

(c) ***Fable:*** A fable is a short fictitious story with a definite moral. In a fable lower animals are invested with human intelligence or motives.

(d) ***Allegory:*** A narrative or a story describing one subject under the guise of another.

3. Figures based on difference i.e. dissimilarity:

(a) Antithesis, (b) Epigram (c) Oxymoron

(a) ***Antithesis:*** This consists in setting contrasted ideas or words against each other for the sake of emphasis e.g. United we stand, divided we fall. To err is human, to forgive divine.

(b) ***Epigram:*** It rouses our attention to some important meaning by using an apparent contradiction. e.g.

i. Cowards die many times before their death.

ii. The child is the father of man.

Since manhood grows out of childhood, the origin of man is a child. A seeming contradiction.

(c) ***Oxymoron:*** Two words of opposite meaning are placed side by side for the sake of a striking effect. e.g.

i. He rose to bad eminence by merit.

ii. The bookful blockhead ignorantly read (Doesn't have right learning).

Other commonly used Figures of speech are:

1. *Personification:* When inanimate objects are given human characteristics, it is known as personification.
2. *Irony:* When a statement or phrase is used to denote an opposite meaning, often a negative or satirical connotation, the figure of speech is called irony.
3. *Apostrophe:* When a character or writer addresses an inanimate object, the figure of speech used is called Apostrophe.
4. *Paradox:* A statement that appears self-contradictory yet true.
5. *Hyperbole:* When over exaggerated phrases are used to emphasize the importance of something it is called hyperbole. E.g. Hamlet in an Act V Scene I says, 'I lov'd Ophelia; forty thousand brothers could not, with all their quantity of love, make up my sum.'
6. *Metonymy:* In this, a word for one thing is used to refer to something related to it e.g. Crown is used to denote the ruler.

Chapter 51

Time-Tested Quotes

Meaningful quotes have the capacity to uplift a person's morale or motivate or inspire a person.

William Shakespeare (1564–1616), one of the greatest playwrights of the world has given some of the best maxims, adages and figures of speech through the versatile characters of his immortal plays. A few samples from his rich, humungous oeuvre:

1. 'Cowards die many times before their death; The valiant never taste of death but once. (Julius Caesar)
2. 'To be or not to be: that is the question:' (Hamlet)
3. 'Be not afraid of greatness: some are born great, some achieve greatness, and some have greatness thrust upon them.' (Twelfth Night)

Considering the burgeoning popularity of English today, let us not forget that Indian authors tried to beat the Englishmen at their own game. English is indeed a window to the world, a truly universal language. Of the renowned Indian personalities who have left an indelible mark as authors and orators in the global scenario, Swami Vivekananda stands tall.

Swami Vivekananda (1863–1902) was a great Indian monk, philosopher and patriot who was proficient in expressing his ideas in fluent English. His address to the august gathering in the Parliament of World Religions in Chicago on 11th September 1893 in his resonant voice, 'Sisters and Brothers of America…' remains a landmark speech where he introduced Hindu Philosophy to the Western World.

A few examples of Swami Vivekananda's inspirational quotes showing his clarity of thought and intellect:

1. 'Arise, awake, stop not till the goal is reached.'
2. 'Strength is life, weakness is death. Expansion is life, contraction is death. Love is life, hatred is death.'
3. 'We are responsible for what we are, and whatever we wish ourselves to be, we have the power to make ourselves. If what we are now has been the result of our own past actions, it certainly follows that whatever we wish to be in the future can be produced by our present actions, so we have to know how to act.'
4. 'They alone live, who live for others.'
5. 'Take up one idea. Make that one idea your life; dream of it; think of it; live on that idea, let the brain, the body, muscles, nerves, every part of your body be full of that idea, and just leave every other idea, alone. This is the way to success, and this is the way great spiritual giants are produced.'

Francis Bacon (1561–1626) an English statesman and philosopher was known as 'The father of English Essays'. Some gems from his essays:

1. Some books are to be tasted, others to be swallowed, and some few to be chewed and digested (Essays: of Studies)
2. Men in great places are thrice servants: Servants of the Sovereign or State, servants of Fame; and servants of Business.... It is a strange desire to seek power and to lose Liberty. (Essays: of Great Place)
3. And he that will not apply New Remedies, must expect New Evils; for Time is the greatest innovator. (Essays: of Innovations)
4. Wives are young men's mistresses; companions for middle age; and old men's nurses. (Essays: of Marriage and Single Life)
5. He that hath wife and children hath given hostages to fortune; for they are impediments to great enterprises, either of virtue or mischief. (Essay: of Marriage and Single life)
6. The joys of parents are secrets and so are their griefs and fears (Essay: of Parents and Children)

7. Travel, in the youngest sort, is a part of education, in the elder, a part of experience (Essay: of Travel)
8. Revenge is a kind of wild justice. (Essay: of Revenge)

Henry David Thoreau (1817–1862): American author, naturalist and philosopher best known for his book 'Walden'. He was a firm believer in 'Transcendentalism' and was believed to have been influenced by the Bhagavad Gita. Some of his immortal quotes are listed below:

1. That man is the richest whose pleasures are the cheapest.
2. As if you could kill time without injuring eternity (Walden).
3. I love a life whose plot is simple.
   And does not thicken with every pimple.
4. The mass of men lead lives of quiet desperation. What is called resignation is confirmed desperation.
5. But it is the characteristic of wisdom not to do desperate things.
6. It is never too late to give up our prejudices.
7. All change is a miracle to contemplate; but it is a miracle which is taking place every instant.
8. There are nowadays Professors of Philosophy but not Philosophers.
9. The morning, which is the most memorable season of the day, is the awakening hour.
10. The Vedas say, 'All intelligences awake with the morning.'
11. To be awake is to be alive.
12. Time is but the stream I go a fishing in.
13. For what are the classics but the noblest recorded thoughts of man?
14. A written word is the choicest of relics.
15. Instead of noble men let us have noble villages of men.
16. I never found the companion that was so companionable as solitude.
17. God is alone, but the devil, he is far from being alone.
18. I had three chairs in my house, one for solitude, two for friendship, three for society.
19. It (Walden Pond) is the gem of the first water which Concord wears in her coronet.

20. I love the wild not less than the good.
21. Goodness is the only investment that never fails.
22. From exertion come wisdom and purity, from sloth ignorance and sensuality.
23. So the coming of spring is like the creation of Cosmos out of chaos and the realization of the Golden Age.
24. However mean your life is, meet it and live it; do not shun it and call it hard names. It is not so bad as you are.
25. Love your life, poor as it is.
26. Superfluous wealth can buy superfluities only.
27. Rather than love, than money, than fame, give me truth.
28. Only that day dawns to which we are awake.
29. The Sun is but a morning star.

CHAPTER 52

Malapropisms

Malapropisms occur when two similar sounding words are interchanged. Malapropism comes from Mrs. Malaprop, a character in Richard Sheridan's play 'The Rivals'. Mrs. Malaprop had the peculiar habit of using words wrongly, confusing them with almost similar words.

Aunt Sally in Huckleberry Finn says, "I was most 'Putrified' with astonishment." It should be 'Petrified'. Another example of malapropism is, "She's as headstrong as an allegory on the banks of the Nile." Here the speaker meant 'Alligator' not 'Allegory'.

CHAPTER 53

Varied Nuances of the English Language

Orthography or the conversational spelling system of a language is thrown to the winds and this can be starkly observed while evaluating English answer scripts of undergraduate and graduate examinees. "Collages, grammer, seperate, fast, leave, giral, hear, quite, defination" are commonly used in place of college, grammar, separate, first, live, girl, here, quiet, definition. On the last page of the answer script one won't be surprised to read 'RUFF DRAUGHT' in place of 'rough draft' intended for precis writing.

Pronunciation becomes the yardstick for most students to write the spelling of words as they sound to their ears. Having attended school and studied in the native tongue, it's not easy to pick up the nuances of English language, unless taught by a good teacher. The unmistakable stamp of the mother tongue obviously, comes to the fore and influences spoken English standards that get reflected in the written style too.

Once, the students of plus two were asked to write an essay on Diwali. The pupil's essay began thus:

'Diwali is a Indian festival. On this day at night dipa laga jaaye. Every house, baana futa jaaye. People wear new dress and eat pitha and sweets. In this way, Deepabali palana kara jaaye.'

Was one to get angry or amused with this hybrid account?

Interpreting the essay was rather tough. 'On the day of Diwali, lamps are lit, crackers are fired and people eat sweetmeats.

In this way, Deepavali is celebrated.'

The transliteration of Odia words into English is common when the pupil finds it difficult to get the equivalent word in English as he or she thinks in the indigenous language and tries to express it in an alien language, almost throttling it. This is not to criticize or humiliate any learner or to harbour any regional bias. On the other hand, the propensity of several students to pick up the rules of grammar, syntax, translate passages and learn the intricacies of the language cannot be undermined. In the Indian context, we cannot overlook the fact that all the States of the Union have been formed on linguistic basis where each language has a rich and varied heritage and literary treasures. A 2018 Census Directorate Report reveals there are 22 scheduled languages and 100 non-scheduled languages in India spoken by one lakh or more people. Renowned scholars opine that the regional languages of our country should break free from the clutches of English hegemony. But the burgeoning globalisation of the Queen's English or American English can never put down the enterprizing spirit of the multi-linguistic, home-based, enthusiastic Indian who hails from different regions and the unmistakable stamp of his local lingo and accent is a huge giveaway. Some words like 'car lifter', 'child lifter', airdash' are typical Indian words in English. Words like carrying (pregnant), stepney (spare tyre), dickey (boot of car), bogie (railway carriage) though obsolete in English are commonly used in India. What is 'lethal' for the British, is 'deadly' for Indians.

Doubts galore keep cropping up in the learner's mind about uttering a word correctly. If 'though' and 'dough' are pronounced similarly then 'cough' ought to be 'co'. If 'cough' is 'coff' why is 'tough' not 'toff' but 'tuff'? Similarly, 'young' sounds like we say it, why do we not spell the organ of taste, the 'tongue' as 'toung'?

Then there are 'silent' letters in a word that shouldn't be pronounced eg. In 'honest' 'h' is silent. 'Heir' is 'air' when uttered; 'Parliament' has a silent 'i'. Why this ambiguity? A forwarded message on social media is appropriate to reproduce here:

The Sound of Silenced Letters

We know the letter B doesn't belong in subtle
But what has the letter C got to do in a muscle?

The role of the D in Wednesday we can't define
Why should G be present in a gnat or in a sign?

To be honest, does the H in rhyme ring a bell?
And can the J in marijuana anybody smell?
Who knows why the K in knee won't knock
And why the L in walk or in calf would not talk.

The first M in mnemonic is hard to understand
Would the damned N in the column ever stand?
We can't say the P in psalm or in psychology
And S alone gets tossed out from the debris.

Is the T heard when you listen to a whistle?
W is not write, it's wrong, don't try to wrestle
X is the mistake in a faux pas, get the clue?
Hush, no rendezvous with Z, goodbye, adieu!

Mere observation suffices to identify the geographical region of the speaker. No innuendoes or derision or offence meant to anyone. If you go to the North, you'll come across treaures (treasures) with plier (pleasure) whatever be the mei-ur (measure) Don't be surprised to hear words like 'school', 'station', 'stamp' being prefixed by 'i' and pronounced as 'ischool', 'istation', 'istamp' or "jobe" instead of 'job'.

Travel eastwards, modern English has a distinct Indian twang where consonants 'v' and 'w' become 'b' or 'bh' and the vowels are rounded off to create new words. So 'vowel' can be 'bhowbel', 'volume' becomes 'bholume' without batting an eyelid.

The western part, comprising mainly Gujaratis exude a distinct drawl while using English words, the most conspicuous one being 'snakes' instead of 'snacks'.

Down South, M, N, S are converted to 'yem', 'yen', 'yes', 'modern' becomes 'morden', 'against' becomes 'again-est'.

Keralites, who are very quick at picking up any language have their own style of uttering English words 'aass' (as), 'co-llege'. However, none can dispute that the mother tongue often has an impact on the accent of the speaker. Learning a language besides one's own mother tongue fosters linguistic harmony among the people of the nation.

An anecdote to be taken lightly is narrated here:

A man entered a garment store and asked the salesman for 'Shaarts'. The salesman scanned the customer from top to toe and asked him, "Are you a Bengali or Punjabi?"

The bewildered customer shot back, "What has that got to do with you?"

With a smile on his face, the salesman declared, "Sir, if you are a Punjabi you mean you want to say 'shorts' but if you are a Bengali, you intend to purchase 'shirts'. I asked in order to figure out what you really meant."

"Oh, got it," laughed the customer.

Jokes apart, many scholars and linguists insist there is nothing called 'perfect' English; even in the West. Today, English is an Indian language as much as the other vernaculars that enrich our linguistic diversity. And the world acknowledges the original writing of authors like the early Indo-Anglian R.K. Narayan, Jawaharlal Nehru, Mahatma Gandhi, Tagore, as well as contemporary greats like Salman Rushdie, V.S. Naipaul, Vikram Seth, Arundhati Roy, Shashi Tharoor, Anita Desai and several others.

It will not be out of place to quote the great South African leader Nelson Mandela's words here, "If you talk to a man in a language he understands, that goes to his head. If you talk to him in his language, that goes to his heart."